Modern Political Analysis

Books by the Same Author

- Theory of Political Sociology (2015)

About the Author

Prof. Shyama Prasad Guru is, at present, an Emeritus Professor of Political Science of Sambalpur University situated at Jyoti Vihar (Burla) in Sambalpur District of the State of Odisha. Born in October 1951, he obtained his Master Degree in Political Science in 1973 from the University of Delhi, and Ph.D Degree from Sambalpur University in 1990. A First Class throughout his academic career, he joined Sambalpur University as a Faculty Member in 1977, and on serving this University for long 35 years, he retired in October 2011 as Professor of Political Science. He specializes in Modern Political Theory and Analysis, Political Sociology, Comparative Politics, and Western Political Thought in the Discipline of Political Science. During his professional career, he has successfully supervised a number of scholars for Ph.D and D.Litt Degrees, and has authored note-worthy research papers and books. Even after retirement, he is actively engaged in teaching and research activities.

Modern Political Analysis
Theories and Models

Shyama Prasad Guru

CONCEPT PUBLISHING COMPANY PVT. LTD.
NEW DELHI - 110 059

ISBN: 978-93-6344-930-5 (HB)
ISBN: 978-93-6344-095-1 (PB)

First Published 2024

Published and Printed by

Concept Since 1974

Concept Publishing Company Pvt. Ltd.
A/15-16, Commercial Block, Mohan Garden
New Delhi-110059 (India)
T: +91-11-41101460
E: publishing@conceptpub.com, *W*: www.conceptpub.com

Cataloging in Publication--Courtesy: D.K. Agencies (P) Ltd. <docinfo@dkagencies.com>

Guru, Shyama Prasad, author.
Modern political analysis : theories and models / Shyama Prasad Guru.
pages cm
Includes bibliographical references and index.
ISBN 9789363440951 (PB)
ISBN 9789363449305 (HB)

1. Political science. I. Title.

LCC JA71.G87 2024 | DDC 320.01 23

Preface

Aristotle, the Father of Political Science, postulates: "Man is a social animal destined by Nature for political life." As such, political life constitutes an integral dimension of the totality of life and existence of the people of every Society. As and when a Society is formed owing to the co-existence of a set of human beings, there emerges the issue of deciding societal goals, and also, the means for attaining them. This necessity for societal decision-making, and the consequent emergence of the Societal Decision-making Apparatus and the concomitant process pave for the formation of the Political Society or the Polity. Since then, from the antiquity to the indefinite future till human beings would live and interact together as members of the Polity, political issues and phenomena have been, and would become the objects of analysis by scholars, intellectuals, and academicians. In these endeavours, 'Modern Political Analysis' occupies a place of special importance, and is of great significance.

Modern Political Analysis connotes analysis of Politics and Political Phenomena on employing Modern Theories and Models designed in Modern (Scientific) Perspective or Approach. Since, in the Discipline of Political Science, the pure-scientific approach is the Behavioural Approach, the Theories and Models designed on the basis of it may be termed as the Scientific Theories, and hence, Modern Political Theories. These Theories and Models provide scientific conceptual frameworks that tend to facilitate systematic academic endeavours for undertaking scientific or modern analysis of political phenomena.

As such, 'Modern Political Analysis' is exclusively concerned with the 'Science of Politics' by way of constituting the foundation for the scientific study and analysis of political phenomena, and of providing relevant scientific orientation and guidelines for undertaking academic endeavours in this context. This branch of knowledge, in the Discipline of Political Science, therefore, is of tremendous importance to the students and researchers who intend to undertake scientific study and analysis of political phenomena. For facilitating these academic endeavours, relevant Theories and Models are required. Of course, in this context, a number of theories are available; however, among them, some very important and most relevant theories which are authored by great scholars, and are incorporated in this Book are: The Decision-Theory of Politics (Harold D. Lasswell); The Power-Theory of Politics (Gaetano Mosca, Vilfredo Pareto, James Burnham, C. Wright Mills, Harold D. Lasswell, Robert A. Dahl); The Group-Theory of Politics (Arthur F. Bentley, David H. Truman, Harry Eckstein); The Systems-Theory of Politics (David Easton, Gabriel A. Almond); The Political-Culture Theory (Gabriel A. Almond, Sidney Verba); The Cybernetic-Theory of Politics (Karl W. Deutsch, Gabriel A. Almond); The Political-Participation Theory (Lester W. Milbrath; and The Political-Development Theory (Lucian W. Pye). This Book also contains an Introductory Chapter that elucidates the Nature, Approach, and Scope of Modern Political Analysis; and an Epilogue that focuses on the limitations of the Behavioural (Modern) Approach, the emergence of the Post-behavioural Approach, and the Contemporary-Trends of Political Analysis.

In preparing this Book, I am immensely benefitted by the wise counsels and inspiration given to me by a number of eminent academicians such as Prof. Sukadev Nanda (Retired Professor of Political Science, Sambalpur University, Odisha), Prof. Satya Narayan Mishra (Retired Professor of Political Science, Utkal University, Odisha), Prof. Arunabho Ghosh (Retired Professor of Political Science, Rabindra Bharati University, Kolkata), Prof. Prakash Chandra Sarangi (Former Professor of Political Science, Central University of Hyderabad, and Former Vice-Chancellor of Ravenshaw University, Odisha), Prof. Arun Kumar Patnaik (Professor of Political Science, Central University of Hyderabad), Prof. G. Ram Reddy (Retired

Professor of Political Science, Osmania University, Hyderabad), Prof. Pralaya Kanungo (Professor of Political Science, Jawaharlal Nehru University, Delhi), Prof. Ashok Acharya (Professor of Political Science, University of Delhi), Prof. Sri Prakash Mani Tripathy (Former Professor of Political Science, Gorakhpur University, Gorakhpur, Uttar Pradesh, and the present Vice-Chancellor of Indira Gandhi National Tribal University, Amarkantak, Madhya Pradesh), and many others. I owe and express my sincere gratitude to all these well-wishers for their kind words and academic support.

I dedicate this Book to my lovely grand-daughters—Akanksha, Eva, Reva, and grand-son Ishaan; and also, to all students and faculty-members of the Discipline of Political Science. If this Book would benefit the students in their quest for advancement of knowledge in Political Science, I would feel immensely rewarded.

Shyama Prasad Guru

Department of Political Science, Osmania University, Hyderabad.

[illegible]

Contents

1

Modern Political Analysis

Nature, Approach and Scope

Political Analysis: the Concept

Analysis involves an intellectual endeavour for undertaking a systematic, logical, and in-depth study of a phenomenon or object. In this process, the concerned phenomenon is, at first, dissected and de-constituted into its constituent parts or elements, and then, each of these parts is subjected to a detailed and rational scrutiny. Finally, the findings obtained on all constituent elements or parts are co-related logically so as to comprehend the nature, structure, and functions of the concerned phenomenon in its totality. This scholarly endeavour, as Vernon Van Dyke[1] points out, thus, involves, resolution of the phenomenon into its component parts, their logical and rational enquiry, and combination and systematization of the findings. As such, the fundamental procedural method of analysis, in general, seems to be the 'Resolutive-Compositive Method'[2] which was originally devised by Euclid, the ancient Greek Mathematician-Cum-Geometrician of the 4th Century B.C., and subsequently followed by Galileo, the

Italian Astronomer of the 16th Century, and many other scholars.

The analysis of a phenomenon may be undertaken in two major, yet different, perspectives such as the 'Qualitative Perspective' and the 'Quantitative Perspective'[3]. The Qualitative Perspective is essentially concerned with the search for 'Value' in analyzing the phenomenon, whereas the Quantitative Perspective is exclusively concerned with the search for 'Fact' concerning it, and it is involved with quantification and measurement of facts. These two perspectives generate and shape two different Approaches such as the 'Normative Approach', and the 'Empirical Approach' to the analysis of all phenomena including political phenomena.

When analysis is undertaken on political phenomena, the academic endeavour may be termed as 'Political Analysis', and as such, 'Political Analysis' may be defined as that intellectual activity which is concerned with the analysis of Politics of a Society. In this academic endeavour, the scholar selects and makes use of a distinct approach, whether the Normative Approach or the Empirical Approach, and proceeds accordingly in his intellectual pursuits. The Approach helps and directs him to devise and design a coherent conceptual framework, what may be termed as a Model or Theory. In general, a Theory may be defined as a coherent framework of ideas (ideals and values) or principles (laws) designed deliberately in relation to a phenomenon for the purpose of understanding and explaining it holistically.[4] It is, indeed, an intellectual enterprise by a human being, and is intended to benefit Mankind in the sense of attainment of the best life and existence for them. As such, 'Political Theory' may be defined as a Theory of Politics designed deliberately for understanding, and also for bettering the Political life and Existence of Mankind. Its relevance is derived from its necessity for the analysis of political phenomena systematically and meaningfully as it provides meaning, coherence and direction to the on-going academic pursuits.[5] However, since an approach for designing a Political Theory may either be value-oriented or fact-oriented, there may be discerned, broadly, two types of Political Theory such as: (i) the Value-Theory, and (ii) the Empirical-Causal Theory.[6] The

Value-Theory presents a framework of values or ideal prescriptions for attainment of the desirable political life for mankind, whereas the Empirical-Causal Theory presents a coherent set of principles or laws for undertaking the analysis of actual political phenomena and issues in order to comprehend and explain the political reality. Both these two types of Political Theory, indeed, enrich the store-house of human knowledge on Politics.

Thus, the nature and scope of Political Theory tend to be shaped and conditioned by an 'Approach' which remains embedded and inherent in the notion or perspective of the scholar on Politics. However, scholars are found to have different and divergent notions on 'Politics', and hence the emanating approaches are found to be many and varied. Yet, there may be discerned two major clusters of notions on Politics on scanning and scrutinizing the definitional discourses. These two major clusters of notions maybe termed as the' Traditional Notion', and the 'Modern Notion' on Politics, and each of these contains and offers a distinct approach which is different from the other. These Approaches are known, in academic arena, respectively as the Traditional Approach, and the Modern Approach which facilitate the formation of the corresponding or concomitant Models and Theories that, indeed, provide guidelines and directions for undertaking systematic and meaningful analysis of Politics. When Political analysis is undertaken on following the imperative of the Traditional Approach coupled with its corresponding Traditional Theory, it may be termed as Traditional Political Analysis; whereas the analysis of Politics which is undertaken on following the imperatives of the Modern Approach coupled with its corresponding Modern Theory may be characterized as the Modern Political Analysis. Since in the process of evolution of Political Analysis, it is found that the type of Modern Political Analysis succeeds the type of Traditional Political Analysis, the nature of Modern Political Analysis may be amply understood and appreciated provided it is distinguished from that of the Traditional Political Analysis.

Traditional Political Analysis

The pattern of Traditional Political Analysis seems to have originated in the notion on Politics conceptualized by Aristotle, the Father of Political Science, in the 4th Century B.C. He was the first scholar to define Politics compactly, and to identify its distinguishing attributes. According to Aristotle[7], the term 'Politics' connotes the affairs of the Polis (State) conducted by the Government in accordance with the provisions of the Constitution for attainment of a life of virtue for its people. This notion contains and presents a distinct approach which requires that the analysis of Politics is to be undertaken in respect of three interrelated dimensions or aspects such as: (i) the provisions of the Constitution which are considered as the fundamental laws of the land, (ii) the conduct of the affairs of the State, in accordance with the provisions of the Constitution, by the Government which is considered as the Agent of the State, and (iii) the attainment of a virtuous life for the people through the functioning of the State and its Government. This approach to Politics, thus, is characterized by the attribute of Legalism as it focuses on the analysis of the fundamental law of the land (The provisions of the Constitution); by the attribute of Institutionalism as it focuses on the analysis of the functioning of the Government (the highest institution or agent of the State); and simultaneously, by the dominant attribute of Normativism as it focuses on the attainment of moral or virtuous life (the value-laden goal) as the ultimate goal of Politics to be realized through the process of policy formulation and implementation in the State. Since this approach with its distinctive attributes emanates from Aristotle's notion conceptualized in the antiquity (in the 4th century B.C.), it is considered as the Traditional Approach. This Approach is found to have been recognized and used by a large number of scholars, from the time of Aristotle to the end of the 19th century A.D., in designing models and theories, and in undertaking the analysis of political phenomena accordingly. Thus, the pattern of 'Traditional Political Analysis' flourished, for about two thousand

and five hundred years, from the 4th century B.C. to the end of the 19th Century A.D.

However, towards the beginning of the 20th century A.D., there emerged dissatisfaction and resentment against the use of Traditional Approach and its concomitant Traditional Models and Theories that produced the traditional patterns of political analysis. These resentments originated as a consequence of the intellectual appraisals on traditional political theories and analysis which were found to be socially irrelevant. These were considered to be the outcome of ivory-tower intellectual exercises, and hence, were essentially formal, legalistic, unrealistic, speculative and normative in nature and consequences.[8] Lacking in reality, these were deficient in solving the actual socio-economic and political problems of mankind, and hence, were socially irrelevant. Therefore, there was felt the need to undertake realistic political analysis on the basis of newly framed realistic political theories and models. In this context, the dissatisfied scholars were inspired and influenced by the then prevalent intellectual tendency of scientism which emerged owing to the achievements of Pure Sciences such as Physics, Chemistry, Mathematics, Biology, and Ecology. Moreover, these scholars were also encouraged by the patterns of modernization and scientification of the Social Sciences such as Economics, Sociology, Anthropology and Psychology which had already incorporated the principles and premises of the Pure-Sciences in their respective academic disciplines. Consequently, the scholars who were interested in the study and analysis of Politics intended to design new political theories and models in conformity with the principles and premises of the Pure-Sciences so as to undertake realistic and scientific analysis of Politics, and thereby, to make their academic endeavours socially relevant. Of course, for designing scientific political theories and models, there was needed a scientific approach inherent in a scientific (realistic) notion on Politics. For this purpose, scholarly endeavours were undertaken in defining Politics realistically that would contain a scientific approach, and would facilitate the formation of scientific or modern theories as deemed necessary for analyzing Politics scientifically and realistically. These scholarly endeavours contributed significantly in inaugurating the new Epoch of Political Analysis which may be termed as the Epoch of Modern Political Theory and Analysis.

Modern Political Analysis

The commencement of the epoch of Modern Political Analysis coupled with Modern Theory-building Activities is found to have impacted significantly the academic endeavours in the discipline of Political Science. Hence, it seems imperative to glance at the (i) Genesis and Nature; (ii) Evolution and Growth; and (iii) Scope and Prime concerns of Modern Political Analysis and Theorization.

Genesis and Nature

The epoch of Modern Political Analysis based and fostered by Modern Political Theories and Models seems to have emerged in the first decade of the 20th Century A.D., specifically in 1908, owing to the pioneering contributions of two great scholars namely, Graham Wallas, and Arthur F. Bentley. Both of them are credited in defining Politics anew, and that too, in conformity with the realism of the Pure Sciences. They rejected and criticized the formalism and normativism of Aristotle's notion on Politics and its inherent Traditional Approach as responsible for the social irrelevance of Political Theory and Analyses. According to them, Aristotle's notion presents the legal-institutional approach which makes political analysis formalistic and superficial; and simultaneously, it offers the normative approach which makes political analysis ideological, speculative, and value-laden. Thus, the Traditional Approach smacks of formalism and normativism, and hence it is unrealistic and unscientific in orientation and perspective. Therefore, both Graham Wallas and Bentley were dissatisfied[9] with the Traditional Approach embedded in the traditional notion on Politics, and they, on being influenced by the realistic approach of the Pure Sciences, defined Politics as a kind of human activity or behaviour actually undertaken in relation to the governance of a

Society. Graham Wallas, in his book 'Human Nature in Politics' published in 1908, postulates that Politics of a Society, in reality, is composed of human actions in relation to the Government, and that these political actions are shaped and conditioned by human psychological instincts and impulses.[10] Hence, he opines that the study of Politics must involve the study of Human Nature because it would "not only deepen our knowledge of political institutions but open an unworked mine of political inventions."[11] Similarly, Arthur F. Bentley, in his book, 'The Process of Government' published in 1908, asserts that the essence of Politics must be found not in the formal constitutional order but in 'the actually performed legislating-administering-adjudicating activities' of the Government of a State.[12] Thus, both Bentley and Graham Wallas, for the first-time, conceptualized Politics as a kind or form of human behaviour in relation the process of governance in a Society. It is a concept that focuses on actual political behaviour while setting aside the legal constitutional framework or the normative goal as the true essence of Politics. Hence, political behaviour must be enquired into, and analyzed for comprehending Politics of a Society in the actual sense of the term. Simultaneously, this perspective considers 'Political Behaviour' as the product of human psychology and sociology, and hence, it necessitates an enquiry into the socio-psychological bases of political behaviour of the individual and the collectivity for comprehending Politics of a Society realistically.

This new notion of Graham Wallas and Bentley is, thus, imbued with realism, and hence scientism and modernism as necessitated by the intellectual need and scientific temper of the time; and it offers a new approach, what may be termed as the 'Behavioural Approach', to political analysis and relevant theory-building endeavours. The Behavioural Approach which emphasizes on realistic and scientific study of Politics is, hence, considered as the Modern Approach; and on being essentially characterized by the principles and premises of the Pure Sciences, it is intended to lay the foundation of the 'Pure Science of Politics'. Since the Behavioural Approach inherent in the conceptualizations of Bentley and Graham Wallas provides a new perspective, for the first time, for undertaking scientific or modern political theorization and analysis, they may be acknowledged as the founding fathers of Modern Political Theory and the concomitant Modern Political Analysis.[13]

Evolution and Growth

With the advent of the 20th Century A.D, specifically from 1908 when Graham Wallas and Bentley presented their new scientific perspective and approach to political analysis, intellectual endeavours were undertaken for designing scientific theories and models for analyzing Politics. Of course, initially, these intellectual endeavours were limited in number because only a few American Scholars subscribed to the behavioural orientation to Politics. However, they provided scholarly encouragement to the behavioural approach to grow and flourish. In this context, Prof. Charles E. Merriam of the University of Chicago (USA), through his work 'New Aspects of Politics'[14] published in 1925, seems to have contributed a lot. Subsequently, the Behavioural Approach to political theorization and analysis was popularized by some behaviourally oriented American Scholars such as Harold D. Lass Well, V.O. Key Jr, David Truman, Herbert A. Simon and other intellectuals, and it was recognized and used subsequently by more and more scholars. However, it was only after the conclusion of the World War II in 1945 that the relevance of the Behavioural Approach was widely recognized by a large number of scholars the world-over, and was used in their intellectual pursuits. For the proliferation and wide acceptance of the Behavioural Approach, the most important cause seems to be the impact of the devastating consequences of the Second World War[15], and the pressing need to solve these challenges. In this context, it may be noted that the Second World War resulted in widespread socio-economic devastations and political changes that included collapse of economic condition of both the victorious and vanquished States, political instability, governmental ineffectiveness, and also, emergence of the scenario of squalor, disease, poverty and social disintegration. Therefore, the most pressing need of the time was to solve these problems of Mankind through the implementation of relevant and realistic schemes of socio-economic reconstruction. For this purpose, plans and schemes were invited from the scholars and academicians. In this context, scholars belonging to various academic disciplines such as Economics, Sociology, Psychology, Anthropology, and Ecology etc. could render substantial contributions, whereas Political Scientists experienced difficulties and inadequacy to design and offer realistic plans and schemes as needed for socio-economic and political reconstruction of the war-damaged States. Consequently, Political Scientists felt impelled to devote themselves to 'self-introspection' and appraisal as to their academic lacunae, limitations and shortcomings. The scrutiny of the hither-to existing researchworks, theories, and models convinced them as to the inadequacy and irrelevance of the Traditional Political Theories and Models, and also, of the deficiency the Traditional Pattern of Analysis for solving the actual problems of the people. As Robert A. Dahl emphatically points out: "The confrontation of theory and reality provoked... a strong sense of inadequacies of the conventional approaches of political science for describing reality, much less for predicting in any given situation what was likely to happen."[16] The enquiry and self-appraisal, thus, provided stimulation and motivation to explore for a new and realistic approach that would exclusively focus on the 'Science of Politics', and would inspire and direct scholarly endeavour to undertake socially relevant analysis of Politics. This intellectual search for a realistic-cum-scientific approach to Politics drew inspiration and insight from the realistic conceptualizations of Graham Wallas and Bentley, and made the 'actual political behaviour of Man', the prime concern for analysis. Thus, the 'Behavioural Approach' which originated in the conceptualizations of Graham Wallas and Bentley was further refined, fostered and fortified by the behaviourally oriented Political Scientists during the period that followed the conclusion of the World War II in 1945. On being considered as the Scientific Approach, and hence the Modern Approach, it was used widely by Political Scientists in designing Scientific Theories and Models, and in undertaking Modern Analysis of Politics. It was this proliferation of the behavioural orientation and persuasion of Politics among the Political Scientists in the aftermath of the conclusion of the Second World War in 1945 that caused the emergence of an academic movement known popularly as the 'Behavioural Movement' in the discipline of Political Science. This movement was pioneered by Prof. David Easton[17] of the University of Chicago (USA), and was nourished and fostered by the intellectual contributions of a large number of American Scholars and Political Scientists including Harold D. Lasswell[18], V. O. Key Jr.[19], David Truman[20], Gabriel A. Almond[21], James S. Coleman[22], G.B. Powell Jr.[23], Myron Weiner[24], David E. Apter[25], Lucian W. Pye[26], Sidney Verba[27], William H. Riker[28], L.W. Milbrath[29], Karl W. Deutsch[30], Robert A. Dahl[31], and many other intellectuals.

The Behavioural Movement

The Behavioural Movement, in the discipline of Political Science, originated as a protest movement in 1945 against formalism (legalism) and normativism of the traditional or conventional approach to Politics. Simultaneously, it was intended to provide a truly scientific foundation to Political theory and Analysis for making academic endeavours socially relevant and useful. As Robert A. Dahl points out, it was "a protest movement within political science"[32] launched by those academicians who shared a strong sense of dissatisfaction with the conventional Political Science, and who believed in the possibilities of improving the study of politics through scientific modes of investigation and analysis. Hence, for focusing exclusively on the 'Science of Politics', the fundamental premises of Pure-Sciences were borrowed; and the scientific principles of factual analysis, objective analysis, and causal analysis were made the guiding principles of political research and analysis.[33] Accordingly, emphasis was accorded to (i) the Principle of Scientific-Empiricism that would require collection of facts (realistic data) on political behaviour of individuals, collectivities, and also incumbents of political institutions of the State through the use of scientific techniques and methods of data collection; (ii) the Principle of Objectivism that would require measurement and quantification of the collected data objectively free from the scholar's values, ideology and preferences, and (iii) the Principle of Causalism that would require scrutiny of these data for finding out the cause-effect-relationship inherent in the political phenomena so as to comprehend these realistically.

Thus, the Behavioural Movement represented the scientific mood or orientation of a group of Political Scientists who assumed that all political phenomena including those of the Government would be stated in terms of observed and observable behaviour of Men, and that these would be scientifically analyzed on following the basic principles of the Pure Science[34] As David B. Truman emphatically points out: "The ultimate goal of the student of political behaviour is the development of a science of the political process."[35] Accordingly, intellectual endeavours were undertaken in conceptualizing Politics with a behavioural orientation and persuasion, and in specifying the attributes of the Behavioural Approach contained therein. In this context, there were conceptualized varieties of scientific notions on Politics. However, among these newly conceptualized notions, that of David Easton seems to be the most coherent, precise, and comprehensive definition which is found to have been accepted as greatly relevant by a large number of scholars in the present time. Easton defines Politics as all those kinds of human behaviour and activities which are undertaken in relation to the entire "process of authoritative allocation of values for a society."[36] As Easton elucidates, the people of a Society form 'values' as preferences on varieties of societal issues such as the desirable patterns of societal organization, societal leadership, societal domestic policies, and societal foreign policies. Their values or preferences on these issues are expressed in the form of demands. Since these demands, in reality, lack unanimity but are conflicting, it becomes necessary to allocate these on resolving the differences of opinions lest the

Society would experience disintegration and instability. Hence, allocations or decisions are made on these conflicting-demands, and that too, authoritatively on backing them with legitimate power and sanctions. In case of disobedience to these authoritative decisions, compliance would be effectively secured and obtained, if necessary, by the exercise of legitimate power involving coercions against the disobedient so that order is established in the Society, and societal stability is ensured. Thus, the Political Process of a Society involves performance of three major, yet interrelated types of activities or behaviour such as: (i) those activities which are concerned with the way values are formed and the value-based demands are transmitted to the Government or Authority for making decisions; (ii) those activities which are concerned with the way the Government (the Authority) makes allocations or decisions in response to the demands; and (iii) those activities which are concerned with the way the authoritative decisions are effectively implemented for ensuring societal stability and viability. All these three major types of behaviour or activities performed actually by the people and the incumbents of the Government in relation to the total process of authoritative allocation of values for a Society, according to Easton, constitute Politics of the concerned Society. Thus, people's behaviour or activities may be termed as Political Behaviour provided it is related to anyone or all these major dimensions of societal politics. This notion of Easton, thus, focuses not only on the political behaviour of the individual and collectivities but also, it includes the political behaviour of the incumbents of political institutions of a Society. As such, Politics is viewed realistically (behaviourally); and simultaneously, the scope of study of Politics is enlarged comprehensively on including within it the dimension of formation and transmission of values and demands, the dimension of enactment of authoritative decisions, and the dimension of effective implementation of these decisions. Moreover, Easton's behavioural notion on Politics postulates that the analysis of political behaviour at the level of the individual, and that of the Society may be meaningfully undertaken provided scientific principles and methods are followed and adhered. Thus, a coherent, realistic, comprehensive and truly scientific notion on Politics is conceptualized by Easton. This definition contains the refined Behavioural Approach which is designed on the premises of the Pure Sciences, and is intended to inspire and guide academic activities for scientific theory-building and modern political analysis.

The Behavioural Approach

The Behavioural Approach is founded on the scientific premise that the study and analysis of Politics must be undertaken on following and adhering to two major principles. These are: (i) the Principle of Value-Fact Dichotomy[37], and (ii) the Principle of S-O-R Co-relationship.[38] The First principle requires that values must be kept separated from political facts in the sense that only observed facts on political behaviour, not the value-judgments on it as to whether it is good or bad, shall constitute the raw material for scientific political analysis and theorization. As Easton points out: "Ethical evaluation and empirical explanation involve two different kinds of propositions that, for the sake of clarity, should be kept analytically distinct."[39] This is imperative because the attainment of reliable knowledge, as Easton[40] emphasizes, may become feasible only if analysis is undertaken on the basis of facts collected and scrutinized through the methods of the Pure Sciences, and that too, free from the personal values and preferences of the researcher. This principle of Value-Fact Dichotomy which must be strictly followed in political behavioural research is also emphasized by Robert A. Dahl when he states: "The empirical political scientist is concerned with what is...not with what ought to be."[41] However, this principle of Value-Fact Dichotomy, Easton[42] opines, does not exclude from scientific analysis the political actor's values and preferences which are to be treated as facts as these tend to determine his political behaviour. Accordingly, realistic facts or data on political behaviour and phenomena are to be collected through observation and the use of other scientific techniques of data collection, and these data are to be measured, quantified and analyzed on using scientific techniques of data analysis. Therefore, in selecting the research problem, and in collecting and analyzing the relevant data on it, the researcher is required to be free from his personal socio-political values. The data, thus objectively collected, would constitute raw material for scientific scrutiny and analysis. As such, there must be ensured complete and rigid separation of the researcher's values from facts in the process of data collection, and simultaneously, the researcher must be value-neutral in analyzing the data.

Moreover, in the process of data-analysis, there must be followed the Second Principle of S-O-R Co-relationship in which 'S' stands for stimulus that causes behavioural responses, 'O' stands for the Organism or the Individual, and 'R' stands for the pattern of his behavioural 'out-put' or responses. As Easton emphatically points out: 'Political Behaviouralism' upholds the paradigm of "S-O-R in which feelings and motivations, and all other aspects of subjective awareness and reactions of the organism are taken into account as potentially useful data."[43] Therefore, the political behaviour of the individual is required to be examined on enquiring into, and identifying the causal stimuli that help generate and account for the pattern of his political behaviour. As such, there is needed to be located and ascertained the pattern of 'Cause-effect Co-relationship' between the actor's emerging pattern of political behaviour and its causal factors or variables. Thus, the two interrelated principles of enquiry and analysis such as the Principle of Value-Fact Dichotomy and the Principle of S-O-R Co-relationship, indeed, make the Behavioural Approach a truly scientific approach characterized by the scientific attributes of factualism, objectivism, and causalism. Consequently, research becomes scientific, and as Easton opines, the Political Scientist is enabled to "describe the way in which people act politically together with the determinants of this activity."[44]

For the convenience of the behaviourally-oriented scholars who undertake empirical-scientific research on political phenomena, Easton[45] specifies and lists eight distinguishing attributes of the Behavioural Approach. These are: 1. Regularities,

2. Verification, 3. Techniques, 4. Quantification, 5. Value-neutrality, 6. Systematization, 7. Pure Science, and 8. Integration. According to Easton, there are discoverable uniformities in political behaviour because the individual tends to display, almost regularly, a distinct and identifiable pattern of behaviour. Hence, while observing the individual's political behaviour, these regularities are to be duly noted by the researcher, and simultaneously, these regular patterns of political behaviour must be ascertained on subjecting these to scrutiny and verification again and again. The verified data are, then, to be collected through the use of scientific techniques of data collection, and are to be quantified and measured precisely with the help of scientific techniques of data-measurement. These academic endeavours must be value-free in the sense of being free from the researcher's personal political values and preferences, and must be undertaken with utmost objectivity. The findings, thus obtained, are to be co-related and analyzed in order to locate and ascertain cause-effect co-relationships that exist between the political behaviour and its causal factors. Consequently, the analysis of political behaviour may be said to take the form of 'Pure-Science', and on the basis of such a scientific study, there may be designed relevant conceptual frameworks, models and theories that would provide guidelines for further research activities. The knowledge on political behaviour, thus obtained, would constitute an integral part of the storehouse of knowledge on 'Human Behaviour'. Since political behaviour is only one distinct dimension of human behaviour, and since it tends to be impacted by all other dimensions of human life, the scientific knowledge on political behaviour, thus obtained, becomes integrated with other branches of knowledge on human behaviour. For the purpose of clarity of understanding of these eight distinguishing attributes of the Behavioural Approach, let us, for example, consider the voting behaviour of the individual as displayed by him in different elections. In the context, the researcher may notice recurrent or regular patterns of voting of a voter in favour of a particular political party in all elections. These regularities need to be ascertained on verifying the

individual's voting pattern in all these elections. Simultaneously, investigations are to be undertaken to find out the causal factors such as psychological, social, economic and other variables that tend to influence the individual to vote for a particular political party persistently or regularly, and accordingly, there must be established co-relationship between his voting behaviour and its determinants. The data, thus obtained and collected, would be quantified and analyzed precisely on using scientific techniques of data measurement and analysis, and that too, free from the researcher's personal political values and preferences. The findings are, then, systematized logically, and basing on these findings, relevant models and theories may be designed. Thus, the analysis of voting behaviour, and the theorization made on it would be akin to 'Pure Scientific Analysis', and the obtained political knowledge would become an integral part of the totality of knowledge on human behaviour.

As such, the Behavioural Approach to Politics may not only facilitate the process of scientific analysis of political behaviour but also, it may direct and foster academic endeavours for scientific-cum-modern political theorization. Thus, socially relevant political analysis and scientific theorization on Politics would reinforce each other. Simultaneously, this interrelationship between theory and research would benefit Mankind in comprehending and solving their actual political problems. As a consequence, the Discipline of Political Science would be greatly enriched, and its relevance would be recognized.

Scope and Prime Concerns

The Scope of Modern Political Analysis and Theory may be delineated in accordance with the prime academic concerns and attributes of the Behavioural Approach. In this context, there may be noted five major academic concerns which tend to shape and characterize the Scope of Modern Political Analysis and Modern Political Theory. These prime academic concerns[46] are: 1. Search for Realism, 2. Search for Comprehensiveness, 3. Search for Universalism, 4. Search for Precision, and 5. Search for Grand Intellectual Orders.

Modern Political Theory-Cum-Analysis is fundamentally concerned with the Search for Realism because it is essentially intended to undertake scientific and realistic analysis of political phenomena. On being characterized by the scientific principle of factualism, its scope rejects values and ideologies, and requires rigid separation of values from facts in order to constitute the factual data as the only basis of political analysis and theorization. It is also concerned with the Search for Comprehensiveness in the sense that realistic data concerning the totality of Politics of a Society including individuals' political behaviour as well as the political behaviour of the incumbents of all political institutions of the Society constitute the raw materials for political analysis and theorization. Moreover, the Search for Comprehensiveness also includes the Search for Universalism in the sense that it encompasses the study and analysis of Politics of all Societies of the World. For this purpose, realistic data on Politics of Societies are to be collected, analyzed, and compared objectively and precisely on employing scientific techniques and methods of data collection and analysis. As such, the Search for Precision in the sense of employment of scientific methods of data collection and analysis is a distinct hallmark of Modern Political Analysis and Theory-building activities. This Search for Precision also requires the scholar's utmost objectivity and value neutrality in selecting the research problems, and in collecting and analyzing the relevant data. Finally, the findings, thus obtained, through the Search for Realism, the Search for Comprehensiveness, the Search for Universalism, and the Search for Precision are to be systematized, and presented in the form of Grand Conceptual Frameworks, Models, and Theories. Thus, all these academic endeavours are ultimately concerned with the Search for Intellectual Orders in the sense of building and designing Models and Theories which would provide guidelines for scientific research activities in the realm of Politics. In this process, theories are verified vis-à-vis the reality of political life and behaviour; and basing on recent findings, the existing theories are either refined, modified, fortified or rejected and new theories are designed. Thus, academic endeavours for political theorization and analysis constitute an ever-continuing intellectual process in which both political analysis and theory-building activities reinforce and foster each other, and contribute to the storehouse of knowledge for the betterment of Mankind.

The academic endeavour for Modern Political Analysis and Theorization are, of course, undertaken on employing the Behavioural Approach to Politics. However, within it, there may be discerned some major perspectives or sub-approaches such as the Decision Approach, the Power Approach, the Group Approach, the Systems Approach, the Political Culture Approach, the Cybernetic Approach, the Political Participation Approach, and the Political Development Approach. These major sub-approaches have facilitated the formation of corresponding Modern Political Theories such as the Decision-Theory of Politics, the Power-Theory of Politics, the Group-Theory of Politics, the Systems-Theory of Politics, the Political Culture Theory, the Cybernetic-Theory of Politics, the Political-Participation Theory, and the Political-Development Theory. These Modern Political Theories and Models tend to provide directions and guidelines to the scholars and researchers for undertaking Modern Political Analysis of political phenomena systematically, scientifically and meaningfully as well.

Notes

1. Vernon Van Dyke (1962). *Political Science—A Philosophical Analysis.* California: Stanford University Press,1960, 2nd Printing, pp. 179-180.
2. C.B. Macpherson (1962). *The Political Theory of Possessive Individualism.* London: Oxford University Press, The Sixth Impression, 1975, p. 30
3. Vernon Van Dyke, *Political Science—A Philosophical Analysis. Op. cit,* p. 180.

4. (i) David Easton. *The Political System—An Inquiry into the State of Political Science*. New York: Alfred A. Knopf. Indian Reprint 1953. Calcutta: Scientific Book Agency, 1971, p. 57.
(ii) Arnold Brecht, *Political Theory*. New Jersey: Princeton University Press, 1959), Indian Reprint (Bombay: The Times of India Press, 1970), p. 14.
(iii) Vernon Van Dyke, Political Science—A Philosophical Analysis. *Op. cit,* pp. 95-96.
5. David Easton, *The Political System. Op. cit,* p. 52.
6. *Ibid.*
7. Aristotle, *The Politics*. Translated by Ernest Barker: *The Politics of Aristotle*; New York: Oxford University Press, Reprint, 1969, p. 1.
8. Heinz Eulau, Samuel J. Eldersveld and Morris Janowitz (eds), *Political Behaviour*. New York: The Free Press, 1956; Indian Edition. New Delhi: American Publishing Co, 1972, p. 7.
9. *Ibid,* p. 7.
10. Graham Wallas (1908). *Human Nature in Politics*. (London: Constable Press.
11. *Ibid.*
12. Arthur F. Bentley (1908). *The Process of Government*. Chicago: Chicago University Press.
13. Heinz Eulau, Samuel J. Eldersveld and Morris Janowitz, *Political Behaviour, Op. cit,* pp. 7-8.
14. Charles E. Merriam (1925). *New Aspects of Politics*. Chicago: Chicago University Press.
15. Robert A. Dahl (1961). "The Behavioural Approach in Political Science: Epitaph for a Monument to a Successful Protest", *American Political Science Review*, No. 55, pp. 763-772, See especially p. 764.
16. *Ibid,* p. 764.
17. David Easton, (i) *The Political System: An Inquiry into the State of Political Science*. New York: Alfred: A. Knopf & Co., 1953. (ii) *A Framework for Political Analysis*. Englewood Cliffs, N.J.: Prentice-Hall, 1965. (iii) *A Systems Analysis of Political Life*. New York: Wiley, 1965.
18. Harold D. Lasswell, (i) *Psychopathology and Politics*. Chicago: Chicago University Press,1930. (ii) *Politics: Who Gets What, When, How*. New York: McGraw Hill, 1936. (iii) *The Analysis of Political Behaviour: An Empirical Approach*. London: Kegan Paul, 1947. (iv) *Power and Personality*. New York: W.W. Norton, 1948. (v) *Power and Society—A Framework for Political Analysis*. New Haven: Yale University Press, 1950) in collabouration with Abraham Kaplan. (vi) *The Decision*

Process: Seven Categories of Functional Analysis. Maryland: University of Maryland Press, 1956.

19. V.O. Key Jr., (i) *Politics, Parties, and Pressure Groups*. New York: Thomas Crowell, 1945. (ii) *Public Opinion and American Democracy*. New York: Knopf, 1961.
20. David B. Truman (1951). *The Governmental Process*. New York: Alfred A. Knopf.
21. Gabriel A. Almond, (i) *The Politics of Developing Areas*. Princeton, N.J.: Princeton University Press, 1960 in collabouration with James A. Coleman. (ii) *The Civic Culture: Political Attitudes and Democracy in Five Nations*. Princeton, N.J.: Princeton University Press, 1963 in collabouration with Sidney Verba. (iii) *Comparative Politics: A Developmental Approach*. Boston: Little Brown & Co., 1966 in collabouration with G.B. Powell, Jr.
22. James S. Coleman, *The Politics of Developing Areas*. Princeton, N.J.: Princeton University Press, 1960 in collabouration with Gabriel A. Almond.
23. G.B. Powell Jr., *Comparative Politics: A Developmental Approach*. Boston: Little Brown & Co., 1966 in collabouration with Gabriel A. Almond.
24. Myron Weiner, *Political Parties and Political Development*. Princeton: Princeton University Press, 1966 in collabouration with Joseph La Palombara.
25. David. E. Apter (1965). *The Politics of Modernization*. Chicago: Chicago Press.
26. Lucian W. Pye, (i) *Communications and Political Development*. Princeton, N.J.: Princeton University Press, 1963 in collabouration with Sidney Verba. (ii) *Political Culture and Political Development*. (Princeton,N.J.:Princeton University Press, 1965. (iii) *Aspects of Political Development*. Boston: Little Brown & Co., 1966.
27. Sidney Verba (1961). *Small Groups and Political Behaviour*. Princeton: Princeton University Press.
28. William H. Riker (1964). *The Theory of Political Coalitions*. New Haven: Yale University Press.
29. Lester W. Milbrath (1965). *Political Participation: How and Why people Get Involved in Politics*. Chicago: Rand McNally Co.
30. Karl W. Deutsch (1963). *Nerves of Government: Models of Political Communication and Control*. New York: The Free Press.
31. Robert A. Dahl, (i) *Who Governs*? New Haven: Yale University Press, 1961. (ii) *Modern Political Analysis*. Englewood Cliff, N.J.: Prentice

Hall, 1963. (iii) *Polyarchy: Participation and Opposition.* New Haven: Yale University Press, 1971.

32. Robert A. Dahl, *The Behavioural Approach in Political Science..., Op. cit.*, p. 766.
33. (i) David Easton, *The Political System—An Enquiry into the State of Political Science, Op. cit.*, p. 66. (ii) Vernon Von Dyke, *Political Science—A Philosophical Analysis, Op. cit.*, p.159, and p. 192. (iii) David Easton, "The Current Meaning of Behaviouralism" in James C. Charles Worth (ed), *Contemporary Political Analysis*, New York: The Free Press, 1967, pp. 19, 25, 31. (iv) David Easton, *A Framework for Political Analysis, Op. cit.*, p. 10.
34. David B.Truman, "The Implication of Political Behaviour Research", *Items*, December, 1951, pp. 37-39.
35. David B.Truman, "The Implications of Political Behaviour Research",' *Items*, December, 1951, Quoted by Robert A. Dahl, *The Behavioural Approach in Political Science. . ., Op. cit.*, p. 767.
36. David Easton, *The Political System: An Inquiry into the State of Political Science, Op. cit*, p. 129.
37. (i) David Easton, *The Political System, Ibid*, p. 53. (ii) David Easton, *A Framework for Political Analysis, Op. cit.*, p. 7.
38. David Easton, "The Current Meaning of Behaviouralism", In James C. Charles Worth (ed.), *Contemporary Political Analysis, Op. cit.*, p. 12.
39. David Easton, *A Framework of Analysis, Op. cit.*, p. 7.
40. David Easton, *The Political System. Op. cit.*, pp. 53, 221.
41. Robert A. Dahl, *The Behavioural Approach. Op. cit.*, pp. 770-771.
42. David Easton, *Ibid.*, p. 221.
43. David Easton, "The Current Meaning of Behaviouralism" in James C. Charles Worth (ed), *Contemporary Political Analysis, Op.cit.*, p. 12.
44. David Easton, *The Political System. Op. cit.*, p. 66.
45. David Easton, (i) *A Framework for Political Analysis, Op. cit*, p. 7 (ii) "The Current Meaning of Behaviouralism" in James C. Charlesworth (ed), *Contemporary Political Analysis, Op.cit*, p. 16.
46. (i) Gabriel A. Almond and G.B. Powell, Jr., *Comparative Politics—A Developmental Approach, Op. cit.*, pp. 6-8. (ii) Dwight Waldo, "Political Science—Tradition, Discipline, Profession, Science, Enterprise" in Fred I. Green Stein and Nelson W. Polsby (eds). *Handbook of Political Science*, Vol. I. *Political Science: Scope and Theory.* London: Addison Wesley Publishing House, 1975, pp. 1-73. (iii) Oran R.Young, *Systems of Political Science.* Princeton, N.J. Princeton University Press, 1968. (iv) Morton R. Davies and Vaughan A. Lewis, *Models of Political*

Systems. London: Pall Mall Press, 1971. (v) Heinz Eulau, *Micro-Macro Political Analysis*. Chicago: Aldine Publishing Co., 1969. (vi) Robert A. Dahl, *Modern Political Analysis*. Engle Cliffs, N.J. Prentice-Hall, 1963. (vii) Ithielde Sola Pool (ed.) *Contemporary Political Science—Toward Empirical Theory*. New York: McGraw-Hill, 1967. (viii) Vernon Van Dyke, *Political Science—A Philosophic Analysis*. Stanford C.A.: Stanford University Press, 1960 (ix) Ronald Young, *Approaches to the Study of Politics*. Evanston, Illinois, North Western University Press, 1958. (x) Arnold Brecht, *Political Theory*. Princeton: Princeton University Press, 1959.

2

Decision Theory of Politics

The Decision-Theory of Politics may be termed as such because it provides a conceptual framework for undertaking the study and analysis of Politics of a Society on focusing exclusively on its decision-making process. Of course, scholars[1] have designed it in different perspectives, and have laid down different variables and parameters. However, the perspective of Harold D. Lasswell seems to be the most useful one because it presents meaningful guidelines for undertaking a comprehensive and scientific analysis of the process of decision-making in a Political Society or State. Its ingredients and variables are found in some of his major works such as 'Psychopathology and Politics'[2]; 'Politics: Who Gets What, When, How'[3]; 'Power and Personality'[4]; 'Power and Society'[5]; and 'The Decision Process: Seven Categories of Functional Analysis'.[6]

Lasswell's Concept of Politics

The founding concept of the Decision-Theory of Lasswell is his basic assumption on 'Politics'. He conceptualized 'Politics' of a Society comprehensively as the mass of activities involved in its 'Decision Process'[7] through which the patterns of distribution of societal values are decided, and accordingly, public policies are enacted and implemented. Therefore, according to him, there may be discerned three major components of the Political Decision-Making Process, and these are: (i) Societal Values, (ii) Enactment of Public Policies, and (iii) Implementation of Public Policies.

Societal Values

Values may be defined as the individual's aspirations and expectations for attainment of desired or preferred objects in life. All these desires of the mass of people of a Society, taken together, constitute 'Societal Values'. As people dwell together and form the Society, they perform activities for producing needs of life, both material and moral, that are necessary for their existence. All these objects pertaining to the needs of life which are produced through inter-individual co-operation are considered by them as valuable objects, and hence these may be termed as 'Societal Values'. They tend to acquire and appropriate these 'Societal Values' on deciding the pattern of distribution as to who would get what, when and how. Since these desired Societal Values are many and varied, for the sake of convenience of analysis, these may be classified, according to Lasswell,[8] into three major categories such as Deference, Income and Safety. The value of Deference implies a desire of the individual for attainment of a higher status in the social hierarchy on acquiring the associated values of Power, Respect, Affection, and Rectitude. On the contrary, the values of Safety and Income mostly involve his desire for personal good and welfare, and these are sought to be attained on acquiring the associated values of Wealth, Well-being, Enlightenment, and Skill.[9] Thus, on the whole, Societal Values may be classified into eight major types such as: Power, Respect, Rectitude, Affection, Wealth, Well-being, Enlightenment, and Skill. In this context, Power is the ability to make and give decisions, Respect involves recognition of intrinsic importance; Rectitude connotes the recognition of inherent morality, Affection involves love and emotional attachment; Wealth refers to possession of material resources, Well-being connotes good health, comfort and safety; Enlightenment refers to wisdom and knowledge; and Skill involves acquisition of special occupational expertise. Each of these values, however, may be considered by the individual either as an 'End-value' or an 'Instrumental Value'. For instance, he may consider 'Power' as an end-value, and may seek to attain it on using 'Wealth' as an instrument or means. Of course, each of these societal values may be used interchangeably, and may be accorded either an end-value or an instrumental-value depending on its perceived importance and relevance. Indeed, the individual, as a member of the Society, desires for and strives to attain these societal values so as to become a Powerful person, Respectable Person, Moral Person, Affectionate Person, Wealthy Person, Healthy Person, Enlightened Person and Skillful Person.

Need for Decision-Making on Societal Values

Since 'Societal Values' are produced through inter-individual co-operation, every member of the Society tends to acquire and appropriate these to the greatest extent possible. However, because of scarcity or lack of abundance of these values, every member is unable to acquire and appropriate these to the best of his aspiration and satisfaction. Hence, there emerges the need for making decision on the pattern of distribution of these societal values for who would get what, when and how. For solving this problem, there is formed a common decision-making apparatus with procedures for deciding the pattern of distribution of societal values among the people. As a consequence, there ensues the societal decision-making process, what may be termed as the political process, through which the pattern of distribution of societal values is decided, and accordingly, public policies are enacted and implemented. The making of public policies and their effective implementation help-establish societal peace and order which, in turn, paves for the Society's growth and development. Hence, the Political Process, understood as the societal decision-making process, constitutes the core-concern of the Society, and it seems to be of paramount importance for societal stability, viability and development.

The Decision-Makers

In the Societal Decision-making Process, ideally, every member is to participate equally with every other in deciding the pattern of distribution of Societal Values. However, in reality, equal participation of each becomes a myth because of inequalities among the people in respect of their biological and intellectual capacities, and material possessions. Consequently, those who are socio-economically and also intellectually superior tend to exercise influence and power over others. These 'Superior Persons' may be termed as the 'Elites'; and because of their superior status, they come to play dominant or key roles in the societal decision-making process in deciding the pattern of distribution of societal values. Since their dominance is caused by their ability to exercise influence and power, these two phenomena are the key determinants of the societal decision-making process.

Both the phenomena of 'Influence' and 'Power' are basically patterns of inter-individual relationships which, in general, involves the controlling ability of an individual or actor over others in achieving the intended objectives on changing the latter's behaviour. However, these two are not identical in essence. According to Lasswell, Influence is an ability which is derived from "the value position and potential of a person or group."[10] and is exercised for "affecting the policies of others than the self"[11] through inducement or persuasion. As different from it, he points out: "It is the threat of sanctions which differentiates power from influence in general. Power is a special case of the exercise of influence, it is the process of affecting the policies of others with the help of (actual or threatened) severe deprivations for non-conformity with the policies intended."[12] Thus, even though, the phenomena of influence and power connote controlling ability of an actor or group to bring about desired changes in others' policies and behaviour, these are different from each other in essence because influence is exercised through the means of persuasion or inducement, whereas Power is exercised through the means of coercion or force. However, both these two types of controlling abilities, indeed, enable an actor or group to become 'The Influential' and 'The Powerful' who may, together, be termed as the Elites of the Society. These Elites who, as such enjoy superior status, become the 'Decision-makers' in the Society, and play dominant and key roles in making and implementing societal decisions.

The Elites, of course, constitute a small numerical minority of the population in a Society. This is because the exercise of influence and power tend to be basically dependent on, and determined by the possession and use of vital resources. Hence, only those persons who monopolize these resources, and have the intention and skill to use these, are capable to control others' behaviour. Since the vital resources, in reality, are found to be unevenly and unequally possessed by the members of a Society because of natural scarcity, and are mostly monopolized by a few persons, there emerges a small group of Elites as the Decision-makers of the Society. Thus, the attainment of elite-status vested with the ability to control the people tends to be determined by three factors such as: (i) Resources, (ii) Intention, and (iii) Skill.[13] In this context, it may be noted that Resources are many and varied. For instance, there are material resources such as money, property and wealth; physical resources such as bodily-strength, well-being and health; and intellectual resources such as intelligence, knowledge, skill and expertise etc. The possession and monopolization of these vital resources tend to accord a person the elite-status because the ability to control others tends to be basically derived from the possession of the resources. However, mere possession of vital resources may help-create the potentiality in a person to become an elite but, in order to play role as an actual elite, he needs to have the necessary intention and skill within him for exploiting and using these resources. Therefore, for becoming an 'Actual Elite', an individual is required to possess not only vital resources but also, additionally, he must have necessary intention and the relevant skill to exploit and use the resources for bringing about intended changes in others' policies and behaviour, and thereby he would secure their compliance. Thus, these three major variables such as Resources, Intention, and Skill[14] conjointly tend to determine the elite-status of an individual, and also his status as to whether he is a 'Political Elite' with the actual capacity to decide and control others. Moreover, within the group of Elites of a Society, the importance of each Elite tends to be determined by the relative amount of his 'Influence' and that of 'Power' which, in turn, are determined conjointly on the basis of his possession of Resources, Intention, and Skill. Therefore, for ascertaining the key-elites who play determining roles in the Decision-making process of a Society, the relative amount of influence and power of each member of the Elite-Group may be empirically measured. Measurement of the amount of influence and power may be undertaken in respects of three major dimensions such as Scope, Domain, and Weight.[15] Scope refers to the number of issues and values on which the Elite is capable of bringing desired changes in others' policies and behaviour by way of using his resources, intention and skill. Domain refers to the number of actors whose policies and behaviour are effectively changed as a consequence of this endeavour. Weight refers to the extent or degree of change in others' behaviour and policies consequent upon the exercise of influence and power by the Elite. Of course, these three dimensions may be enquired into conjointly for measuring and determining the amount of influence and power of an elite, and for ascertaining his status and importance in the Societal Decision-making process. For instance, the greater is the scope, the domain and weight of his influence and power, taken together, the greater may be his status as an Elite. Accordingly, there may be identified a group of Core-Elites who, in reality, play determining role in deciding the pattern of distribution of societal values. Their decisions come out in the form of Public Policies which are authoritatively implemented in the Society. Thus, the group of Core-Elites tends to function as the group of actual decision-makers, and it constitutes the pivot on which the entire Decision-making Process of the Society revolves.

The Decision-Process

The Decision-making Process through which the pattern of distribution of societal values is decided, and public policies are enacted by the Elites involves, according to Lasswell, performance of seven major types of functions. These are the function of: (1) Intelligence, (2) Recommendation, (3) Promotion, (4) Prescription, (5) Invocation, (6) Appraisal, and (7) Termination.[16]

In the Decision-making Process, while enacting Public Policies, the first and foremost function that must be performed is the Intelligence Function. Its performance involves collection of relevant information and data on the intended policy to be enacted. For the purpose of comprehension, let us, for instance, consider the process of enactment of Health Policy. For its enactment, there need to be collected initial and primary information on the issue of the physical well-being and health care of the people in its multifarious dimensions such as the number of people who are afflicted or likely to be afflicted by various types and kinds of diseases, the number of hospitals with physical infrastructures such as buildings and instruments needed for this purpose; the number of Doctors and para-medical personnel necessary for treating the patients; the types and quantity of medicines needed and to be produced by the pharmaceutical companies; the number of Medical Colleges to be established for producing and training Doctors and Medical Professionals, and finally making an estimation of the financial resources required for attainment of the goal of health care effectively. These primary information and data would constitute the raw material for making and designing policy proposal on the intended Health Policy. The performance of this initial Function of Intelligence is to be followed by the performance of the second Function of Recommendation that involves making of alternative policy-proposals on the concerned issue along with relative pros and cons, cost and benefit, and advantages and disadvantages of each proposal. From among these alternative policy-proposals, only one proposal is to be selected rationally on comparing these, and that one is to be selected which is assessed to be the best one for realistic attainment of the intended goal. This function of selecting the best feasible one among the recommended alternative policy-proposals is called as the Function of Promotion. It is followed by the performance of the Function of Prescription that involves the enactment of relevant laws, rules and regulations, in detail, as required for effective implementation of the concerned Public Policy. Soon after the Policy becomes enacted, there takes place its implementation, and this function of implementation is called as the Function of Invocation. After implementing the Policy for some reasonable time, it needs to be evaluated and assessed for finding out the extent of attainment of the intended goal as well as the problems and difficulties that are experienced during its implementation or invocation. This function of evaluation is termed as the Function of Appraisal that brings to light the drawbacks and shortcomings of the invoked public policy, and that contains suggestions for the required amendments in it or abrogation of it. Accordingly, for effective attainment of the intended goal, necessary modifications or abrogation of the concerned public policy would be made; and this function is termed as the Function of Termination. Thus, the Decision-making Process through which the pattern of distribution of societal values is decided, and policies are enacted and implemented involves necessarily the performance of these seven major types of functions. In this context, the Societal Values constitute the 'What' of the Decision-making Process, whereas its 'Who', 'Where', and 'How' are determined by the Core-Elites or Decision-makers of the Society.

Political Implications of Public Policy

The Elites, as the Decision-makers of a Society, constitute the Government; and they, in reality, enact and implement Public Policies so as to establish and maintain socio-political order, stability and viability. However, attainment of this goal tends to be crucially determined by their effectiveness which, in turn, tends to be dependent upon the extent of peoples' legitimacy. In this context, it may be noted that legitimacy is the belief-system of the people that the Government and its policies are proper and just, and hence, are legitimate and to be obeyed. It is this positive attitude and favourable disposition of the people towards the Government and the Public Policies that tend to generate in them spontaneous willingness to render obedience and legitimacy. It is this sense of legitimacy that motivates the people to support and obey the Government and its policies willingly; and as a consequence, Public Policies are effectively implemented paving for, and ensuring the attainment of socio-political stability and viability. Of course, public policies may be effectively implemented and peoples' obedience may be secured through the exercise of power involving coercion, but such obedience of the people obtained through coercion, and devoid of spontaneous legitimacy would not last long, and would not make for durable stability for the Government, because 'Will', 'not Force' is the basis of State. Since effectiveness of the Government depends mostly upon legitimacy of the people, the Ruling Elites use measures for generating legitimacy besides using power and coercion for securing people's obedience; and hence, they tend to devise relevant strategies basing on Symbols, Practices, Skill, Goods, and Violence.[17] For convenience of comprehension and analysis, these may be broadly classified as Ideological, Diplomatic, Economic, and Military Strategies.[18] The Ideological Strategy focuses on the symbols of common identity and a bright destiny for an utopian Polity; it also focuses on relevant practices and procedures of governance and administration concerning the projected goal. The Diplomatic Strategy contains skilfully designed means of persuasion and inducement for obtaining and securing peoples' willing compliance to the Elite-rule on presenting it as beneficial to the people. It aims at creation of favourable disposition in the people towards the Government through cleverly designed peaceful but manipulative techniques such as publicity, propaganda, media-communication, educational system, and agents of socialization including various social and political groups. The Economic Strategy involves enactment of economic policy on planning the economic resources of the Society so as to make the people feel that the Government is economically beneficial and advantageous to them. These three strategies such as the Ideological, the Diplomatic, and the Economic Strategies are peaceful strategies which are intended to generate and foster legitimacy in the people in favour of the Government; whereas the fourth one, the Military Strategy is concerned with the use of State-Power (Coercion) including deployment of Military and Police Forces, in the event of failure or inadequacy of the peaceful strategies, for securing peoples' obedience on forcefully suppressing their resentment. Thus, the peaceful strategies involve the exercise of influence, whereas the Military strategy involves the exercise of power by the Ruling-Elites for securing people's compliance, and for ensuring stability of the Government. In this context, however, Lasswell opines: "Violence must be subordinated to the total operation of which it is a part"[19] and "Special attention must be given to social change... for effectiveness."[20] Thus, according to him, too much reliance and emphasis must not be accorded to the use of Military Strategy and Coercive Measures because these may create deep-rooted resentment and widespread alienation in the people against the Government, and may cause revolt and political instability. On the contrary, greater emphasis needs to be accorded to the employment of peaceful persuasive strategies for creating favourable disposition and legitimacy in the people towards the Government so that it may enjoy durable and effective stability through time. As Lasswell emphatically points out: "The ascendancy of an elite depends in part upon the successful manipulation of its environment."[21] Thus, for creating legitimacy in the people, and retaining their spontaneous support, Lasswell requires the Government to keep the people satisfied on enacting public policies which would be perceived by them as beneficial; and also, if necessary, on suitably modifying its structure and policies, and bringing out social changes as desired by the people. Thus, Lasswell recognizes the pressing need for legitimacy as a prerequisite for maintaining and retaining governmental stability; and simultaneously, for obtaining people's legitimacy, he requires the Government to keep the people satisfied on bringing about necessary socio-political changes, from time to time, as desired and demanded by them.[22]

A Critical Appraisal

Lasswell's Decision-Theory of Politics, on close scrutiny, seems to present an undemocratic and illiberal theorization of the Political Process of a Society because it ignores the essential democratic values of popular participation and responsible Government. He does not present the people as the Sovereign Authority; rather he assigns sovereignty to the Ruling-Elites who decide all societal issues and values, and impose their decisions through the exercise of influence and power. In Lasswell's Model, people remain as a large group of influencees and the power-addressees, whereas a small group of Ruling-Elites becomes the Influencer and the Power-holder. People give obedience to the Ruling-Elites, and are denied any effective participation in deciding the pattern of distribution of societal values that comes out in the form of public policy. Hence, people are denied political liberty and equality of participation in the societal decision-making process; they are deprived of sovereignty, and they are presented as powerless non-entities in the political process. On the contrary, the status and role of the Ruling-Elites are eulogized as the Decision-makers of the Society, and they are considered as instrumental for attainment of societal stability and development. Hence, Lasswell's perceptions amount to an elitist-theorization of the political process. Simultaneously, this Theory seems to be characterized by in-egalitarianism because the pattern of distribution of societal values by the Ruling-Elites would inevitably be more advantageous and beneficial to them as against the people who are powerless, and deprived of participating equally and effectively in the decision-making process. As the Elites are the decision-makers, they would appropriate greater societal resources and values which would be used by them to perpetuate themselves as the Society's Decision-makers through time at the cost of the people as a whole.

Moreover, Lasswell's Theory seems to be self-contradictory and confusing. This is evident in his theorization that the Ruling-Elites, for ensuring governmental stability and effectiveness, must obtain people's legitimacy. If the Ruling-Elites are the decision-makers because they are men of power, why would they require people's legitimacy to make their rule stable and effective? If Elites are powerful and people are powerless, as Lasswell presents, why would the powerful elite require people's willing obedience or legitimacy for effective implementation of public policies without exclusively depending on the use of coercion? Are the Elites powerful or the People powerful? How can both the parties, —the Elites and the Mass of People, be powerful in the Society simultaneously? Thus, Lasswell's presentation of the group of the Ruling-Elites as the powerful group of persons in the societal decision-making process, and simultaneously, his recognition of the importance of people's legitimacy as the basis of governmental stability contain an element of contradiction and confusion in his theory.

These shortcomings, however, do not reduce the importance of Lasswell's Decision-Theory of Politics; rather his contributions are immense to the realm of Modern Political Theory and Analysis. In designing his theoretical construct, his perspective is empirical and it is not status-quoist but development-oriented as he is in favour of equilibrium (stability) with social changes. Indeed, it is his pioneering academic endeavour in designing a realistic conceptual framework for undertaking scientific and developmental analysis of the Political Process that has placed him in the first rank as a Modern Political Theorist.

Notes

1. (i) Herbert A. Simon and C. Barnard (1947). *Administrative Behaviour.* New York: Macmillan. (ii) W.E. Moore (1953). *Organizational Behaviour* (Princeton, N.J : Princeton University Press. (iii) Richard C. Synder, H.W. Bruck, and Burton Sapin (1954). *Foreign Policy Decision-Making: An Approach to the Study of International Politics.* Princeton, N.J: Princeton University Press.
2. Harold D. Lasswell (1930). *Psychopathology and Politics.* Chicago: Chicago University Press.
3. Harold D. Lasswell (1936). *Politics: Who Gets What, When, How.* New York: Mc-Graw-Hill.

4. Harold D. Lasswell (1948). *Power and Personality*. New York: W.W. Norton and Company.
5. Harold D. Lasswell & Abraham Kaplan (1950). *Power and Society: A Framework for Political Inquiry*. New Haven, CT: Yale University Press.
6. Harold D. Lasswell (1956). *The Decision Process: Seven Categories of Functional Analysis*. College Park, Maryland: University of Maryland Press.
7. Harold D. Lasswell (1951). *Politics: Who Gets What, When and How*. In Political Writings of Harold D. Lasswell. Compiled and Reprinted by the Free Press, Glencoe (Illinois), p. 295.
8. *Ibid.*, p. 295.
9. Harold D. Lasswell, "Democratic Character", in *Political Writings of Harold D. Lasswell, Op. cit.*, pp. 474-80.
10. Harold D. Lasswell & Abraham Kaplan, *Power and Society, Op. cit.*, p. 55.
11. *Ibid.*, p. 71.
12. *Ibid.*, p. 76.
13. *Ibid.*, p. 71.
14. *Ibid.*, p. 73.
15. *Ibid.*, p. 71.
16. Harold D. Lasswell, *The Decision Process: Seven Categories of Functional Analysis. Op. cit.*, pp. 2-23.
    Also, Harold D. Lasswell (1963). *The Future of Political Science*. New York: Atherton Press, pp. 15-16.
    Harold D. Lasswell (1971). *A Preview of Policy Sciences*. New York: Elsevier Publishing Company.
    Harold D. Lasswell (1971). *The Policy Orientation of Political Science*. Agra, India: Lakshmi Narayan Agarwal Press, p. 23.
17. Harold D. Lasswell, *Politics: Who Gets What, When, How, Op. cit.*, pp. 311-391.
18. Oran R. Young (1968). *Systems of Political Science*. Englewood Cliffs, N.J.: Prentice Hall, Inc, p. 69.
19. Harold D. Lasswell, *Politics: Who Gets What, When, How, Op. cit.*, p. 340.
20. *Ibid*, p. 341.
21. *Ibid*, p. 444.
22. *Ibid*, p. 445.

3

Power Theory of Politics

Power-Theory is concerned with the study and analysis of Politics or Political Process of a Society focusing exclusively on the interplay of legitimate power within it. Its fundamental assumption is that Power is the defining attribute of Politics because a Polity or Political Society may be broadly defined by some eminent Political Theorists including Robert A. Dahl as "any persistent pattern of human relationships that involves, to a significant extent, power, rule or authority."[1] Hence, scholars[2] who subscribe to this notion conceptualize the Power-Theory as a framework for undertaking substantive empirical analysis of the Society's Political Process on comprehending it as the Power-Process of the Society.

The Concept of Power

The term 'Power', in general, connotes a pattern of inter-individual relationship characterized by the ability of an Actor to bring about intended changes in the behaviour and policies of others through the exercise of coercion.[3] For instance, there may prevail a pattern of inter-individual relationship, at the minimum, between two Actors such as 'A' and 'B' and, in their relationship, 'A' intentionally undertakes an endeavour to effect intended changes in 'B's behaviour and policies. While doing so, 'A' would use his resources against 'B' in order to coerce him physically or psychologically to change his behaviour and policies; and consequently, 'B' is coerced to change himself as desired by 'A'. The success of 'A' in effecting intended changes in 'B's behaviour establishes a power-relationship between them. In this context, 'A' becomes the Power-holder, and 'B' becomes the Power-addressee. In this power-relationship, the Power-addressee changes his behaviour and policies as desired by the Power-holder because of actual loss caused, or fear of prospective loss for non-compliance. It is the consequence of actual loss or the fear of prospective loss that coerces or forces the Power-addressee either physically or psychologically to comply with the desire and directions of the Power-holder. As Robert A. Dahl emphatically points out, power relationship necessarily involves "severe losses for non-compliance."[4] Therefore, for exercising Power, an Actor needs to possess vital resources, and exploit these resources intentionally and skilfully for coercing other actors to render compliance on causing actual loss or deprivations to them, or creating in them the fear of prospective loss or deprivations.

This general notion on Power seems to provide motivation to scholars to design a conceptual construct for analyzing the political process of a Society in which there prevails a distinct pattern of legitimate power relationship between the Government and the Governed. The Government which is the legitimate Decision-making Structure of the Society is composed of Men of Power; and they may be termed as the Ruling-Elites because they are empowered to make decisions on all societal issues. The power of these Elites flows from the vital resources possessed by them; and the actual exercise of Power takes place because of their intention and skill in exploiting these resources for securing compliance of the people and if necessary, on coercing them. Simultaneously, the Elites also cleverly induce the people (the Power-addressee) to legitimize the Elite-rule and to comply peacefully to the decisions of the Ruling-Elites. Thus, there is formed a distinct pattern of legitimate power relationship between the Government which is composed of the Ruling-Elites, on one hand, and the people who are ruled, on the other. Accordingly, the Political Power-Structure of the Society emerges with a distinct shape and form.

Society's Political Power-Structure

The emerging pattern of legitimate power relationship between the Ruling-Elites and the People is sought to be maintained and stabilized on designing a suitable Governmental Structure, what may be termed as the Political Power-Structure of the Society. Of course, since the Government is composed of the Elites who are, as such, the holders of legitimate power, the Political Power-Structure becomes, inevitably, elitist in form. However, the dynamics of this Elitist Political Power-Structure tends to be crucially determined by the pattern of interrelationship among the Ruling-Elites who constitute the Government at a given time. Hence, a meaningful analysis of Politics or Political Process of a Society seems to necessitate an enquiry into the pattern of its Political Power-Structure. For undertaking such empirical enquiry and analysis, Researchers may make use of two major, yet different, Models as designed by eminent scholars, and these are named by Geraint Parry[5] as: (i) the Monolithic-Pyramidal Model, and (ii) the Pluralistic-Polyarchal Model.

The Monolithic-Pyramidal Model

The basic hypothesis of the Monolithic-Pyramidal Model is that the Society's Political Power-Structure is composed of a single, cohesive group of Ruling-Elites, and hence, the legitimate Political Power of the Society is unicentric in the sense that there is a single centre of legitimate power in it. The Ruling-Elites who constitute the Political Power-Structure are a small numerical minority of influential and powerful persons; and they, together, make authoritative decisions on all issues of the Society. Their decisions are obeyed habitually by the people of the Society because of fear of force, or a belief in the goodness of the Ruling-elites. This small group of Ruling-Elites, despite its smallness in size and number, however, cannot be controlled by the people because of its unity and cohesiveness. As James Meisel[6] points out, the Ruling-Elite Group is capable of maintaining its dominance over the people because it is characterized by 3 C's such as: (i) Consciousness , (ii) Cohesion, and (iii) Conspiracy. The Elites are conscious of their superior status, and they have a common conscious 'Will' to maintain and perpetuate themselves as the decision-makers of the Society through time. Their common consciousness generates unity and cohesion among them, and motivates them to work together actively with strong determination to realize the cherished objective on devising and implementing required strategies. Hence, they also tend to be conspiratorial in intention and action. Thus, the Ruling-Elites constitute a small cohesive group of persons who exercise legitimate power, and hence, Society's legitimate power becomes unicentric.

From this basic hypothesis, there may be derived and noted some distinguishing features of the Monolithic-Pyramidal Model. These are:

1. Society's Political Power-Structure is essentially monolithic in form because its legitimate power remains centralized, and hence, concentrated in a single small group of persons.
2. The small group of the Ruling-Elites constitutes the Political Power-Structure, and it makes authoritative decisions on all issues of the Society.
3. The Group of Ruling-Elites always presents itself as a highly cohesive group because of the common consciousness, determination, and strategies of its members to perpetuate them as the Society's Decision-makers through time.
4. The Power of the Ruling-Elite Group is cumulative in the sense that power is used to increase power through greater accumulation and clever exploitation of vital resources.
5. The Society's Power-Structure is not only monolithic but also pyramidal in form because it is broad at the base, and pointed at the top. This Pyramidal-Structure emerges because the Ruling-Elite Group, in reality, is composed of two strata of Elites such as the stratum of actual or

core decision-makers who are only a few persons, and the stratum of potential decision-makers who are relatively more in number. Both these strata of Ruling-Elites, of course, work together as a single united cohesive group of Decision-makers.

These distinguishing features, on the whole, tend to characterize the Monolithic Pyramidal Model of Society's Political Power-Structure. However, within this general framework, there may be noted divergent perspectives among the Elite-Theorists as to the key to elite-domination and control in the Society. In this context, four major perspectives[7] may be discerned; and these are: (i) The Organizational Perspective , (ii) The Psychological Perspective, (iii) The Economic Perspective, and (iv) The Institutional Perspective.

The Organizational Perspective

The Organizational Perspective is the viewpoint of two great scholars such as Gaetano Mosca and Robert Michels. However, both of them differ from each other in their respective Organizational Perspective. Mosca, in his book 'The Ruling Class'[8] asserts that, in every society, the Ruling-class composed of Men of Influence and Power is numerically a small group of persons, and that, despite its numerical smallness in size, it is capable of maintaining and perpetuating its dominant status owing to its superior organizational ability. He points out: "The power of any minority is irresistible against each single individual in the majority who stands alone before the totality of the organized minority."[9] The Ruling Class of Elites always presents itself as a highly cohesive group; and its cohesiveness is derived from the common consciousness and determined 'Will' and action of its members to keep themselves as the Society's Decision-makers. Thus, the Ruling-Elites are capable of organizing themselves as a close-knit group. On the contrary, the Ruled-class composed of the mass of people stands thoroughly disorganized as a large aggregation of single, isolated individuals with no common consciousness and will to action. Therefore, according to Mosca, the organized Ruling-class of Elites takes advantage of the disorganization and disunity among the people; and it rules over the people on exercising influence and power through time. Thus, Mosca traces the key to the domination and control of the Ruling-class of Elites to its superior organizational ability.

As different from Mosca, a different organizational perspective to the Elite-Rule in the Society is presented by Robert Michels who, in his book 'Political Patties'[10] accounts for elite-dominance over the people to the organizational necessity of the Society. According to Michels, for the Society to exist and survive through time, it needs to be organized in the sense that its goals must be decided, and accordingly, public policies must be enacted and implemented effectively in order to realize the decided goals, and also to establish order for avoiding anarchy. Of course, for making decisions on all these societal issues, and implementing these effectively, there is needed intellect, talent and intelligence which, however, are naturally found inherent in a few individuals, whereas the people, in general, are found to be amateur, indolent and indifferent. Thus, in the Society, leadership qualities are found naturally vested in a few intellectually superior, talented, and clever individuals who become the Ruling-Elites, and they take the advantage of the peculiar psychology of the mass-mind for perpetuating their domination and rule over the indolent, indifferent, and ignorant people. Therefore, Michels traces the key to the elite-domination and rule in the Society to the technical indispensability of the leadership of the Elites for the maintenance and survival of the Society on fulfilling its organizational needs; and he emphatically asserts: "Who says organization, says oligarchy."[11]

The Psychological Perspective

The Psychological Perspective is hypothesized by Vilfredo Pareto[12] who in his book "Mind and Society" traces the key to Elite-rule in the Society to the psychological traits or instincts of the Elites and the Non-elites. He terms these psychological traits as 'Residues' and classifies these into two broad categories such as 'Class-I Residue', and 'Class II Residue'. According to him, 'Class-I Residue' is characterized by imaginative and speculative tendencies which are akin to Fox-like qualities, and make Man intelligent, clever and cunning, whereas 'Class-II Residue' is characterized by a tendency for maintenance of order, discipline and stability which are akin to Lion-like qualities. Both these two types of Residues are present in every individual but in different proportions from person to person. As such, predominance of 'Class-I Residue' makes a person a clever and cunning individual like a Fox, whereas predominance of 'Class-II Residue' generates in him lion-like propensities and dispositions for order, stability and material development. As Pareto observes, the psychology of the mass of people is mostly characterized by 'Class-II Residue' (Lion-like qualities); but among the Elites (Men of Influence and Power), there are some persons with the predominance of 'Class-I Residue' (Fox-like qualities) and some persons with the predominance of 'Class-II Residue' (Lion-like qualities). Thus, there are two groups of Ruling-Elites such as the Group of Foxes and the Group of Lions, whereas the people lack in intelligence but usually desire for order, stability, and material development; and hence they tend to depend upon the Elites as they need their leadership for enactment of public policies. The need for material development is addressed when the Ruling Group of Fox-like Elites enact and implement public policies on using their talent and intellect, but they, because of their timidity, refrain from using force to maintain order and stability. Consequently, their rule lapses into anarchy. Since the maintenance of socio-political order is necessary for the survival of the Society, the Group of Lion-like Elites take advantage of the situation, organize revolt, and violently overthrow the Ruling Group of Fox-like Elites. Thus, the Government becomes constituted of the Lion-like Elites who firmly establish socio-political order and stability, but since they lack in the required intellectual ability to devise policies for bringing about people's economic development, there emerges dissatisfaction against the Government. Hence, for assuaging people's discontent, the Ruling-Group of Lion like Elites invites and allows entry of some intelligent Fox-like Elites into the Government for devising policies of economic development. Thus, the intelligent and clever Fox-like Elites gradually enter into the Power-Structure, and they replace the then existing Ruling Group of Lion-like Elites. Therefore, Pareto presents his Theory of Circulation of Elites and hypothesizes that there takes place constant alternation or circulation between the two Groups of the Ruling-Elites such as the Group of Lion-like Elites and the Group of Fox-like Elites; and that the style of governance, at a given time, seems to be characterized correspondingly by the psychological traits of these two Group of the Ruling-Elites. Moreover, Pareto postulates that the stability of the Government tends to be crucially determined by the peculiar patterns of psychological traits and properties of these two groups of Ruling-Elites as well as the Mass of People.

The Economic Perspective

The Economic Perspective is presented by James Bumham[13] in his book 'The Managerial Revolution'. He identifies the economic factor as the key to the elite-domination and control in the Society, and postulates that economic power paves for political power.

According to him, the Managers of the major means of production, in reality, become the Elites with economic power, and hence, these Managerial Elites become the Ruling-elites. He notices the emergence of the Capitalist Class as the Ruling-class of the Society from the time of the advent of the industrial revolution because of its ownership and control of the major means of production. However, in the contemporary time, the Capitalist Class has remained merely as the owner of the means of production, whereas the actual control and management of the production-process have been transferred to the Managerial-Elites because of their specialized skill and expertise. It is this indispensability of technical and managerial knowledge for modernizing the production-process that places the Managerial-Elites as its actual managers and controllers. Hence, according to Burnham, this Professional-Class enjoys not only economic power but also actual decision-making power in the Society as governance also involves the use of technical and professional knowledge and expertise. Thus, Burnham traces the key to the Elite-Rule in Modern Society to the technical and professional indispensability of the Managerial Elites.

The Institutional Perspective

The Institutional Perspective is hypothesized by C. Wright Mills[14] in his work 'Power Elite' in which he traces the key to the Elite-Rule to the major strategic institutions of the Society. He postulates that power resides in, and flows from the key institutions, and hence, those who hold top positions or command-posts in strategic institutions of the Society become powerful, in reality, in making and enforcing societal decisions. For vindicating this thesis, he enquires into the political decision-making process in the USA, and locates the actual decision-makers in three major or key institutions such as the Military, the Big Corporations, and the Political Executive. He notices strong interconnections among these key institutions, and also among the leaders who hold command positions therein. These leaders constitute a coherent group of powerful persons, and decide all major issues and policies in the American Society. They are termed by C. Wright Mills as the 'Power-Elites' who constitute a cohesive group of actual decision-makers. Thus, he traces the key to the Elite-Rule to the institutional landscape of the Society.

Perspectival Diversities and Consensus

The scholarly perspectives of the Monolithic-Pyramidal Model of the Society's Political Power-Structure reveal significant diversities as to the key to the Elite-Rule in the Society. Mosca traces it to the organization ability of the Ruling-Elites, Michels finds it in the organizational necessity of the Society, Pareto traces it to the patterns of psychology of the Ruling-Elites and the People; Burnham finds it in the management and control of the production-process; and C. Wright Mills locates it in the institutional land-scape of the Society. However, despite these diversities, all of them unanimously assert that the Society's Political Power-Structure is Monolithic-Pyramidal in form because it is composed of, and operated by a single Ruling-Elite Group which is pointed at the top but broad at the base.

The Pluralistic-Polyarchal Model

The basic premise of the Pluralistic-Polyarchal Model is that the Society's Political Power-Structure is elitist but, in reality, poly-centric and decentralized in form. This Model is the intellectual product of some distinguished Power-Theorists such as Arthur F. Bentley[15], Joseph A. Schumpeter[16], David Truman[17] and Robert A. Dahl.[18] who hypothesize that the Society is structurally composed of a plurality of Groups with different and divergent interests, objectives, and resources; and that each of these Groups is represented and led by its own leaders who may be termed as the Elites. These Groups differ from one another in respect of form, size, objective, intensity, and effectiveness because of differences in their bases or vital resources such as wealth, knowledge, and wisdom, skill and expertise, physical prowess, and charisma etc. These resources are not monopolized by a single group but are unevenly possessed by a plurality of groups. Hence, Society becomes pluralistic in structure. However, every Group is led by its own leaders who are persons of influence and power, and as such, they are termed as its Elites. These Elites of various Groups seek to protect and promote their own interests as well as respective group interests while playing their roles in the Societal Decision-Making Process. Hence, because of diversities of interests of the Elites of these various groups, they do not constitute a single cohesive Group of Decision-makers. Consequently, Society's Power-Stmcture becomes poly-centric and de-centralized; and simultaneously it becomes polyarchal because policy-decisions are made by the Elites of different Groups of the Society amidst competition, conflict and cooperation among them. Thus, there prevails Elite-rule in the Society as its Decisions-makers are the Elites, and people render obedience to their decisions. However, decision-making power is not centralized but dispersed among the Elites of these various Groups. Of course, the Elites, in order to maintain and perpetuate their superior status, tend to work cleverly in exploiting their resources for persuading and convincing the people as to their goodness and benevolence. Thus, they seek people's approval and legitimacy to the Elite-rule through periodic elections on employing the strategies of persuasion, publicity, and propaganda. As such, the Political Power-Structure of the Society, in reality, becomes Pluralistic-Polyarchal in form, and is characterized by the principle of Democratic-Elitism.

A Critical Appraisal

These two Models such as the Monolithic-Pyramidal Model and the Pluralistic Polyarchal Model present divergent hypotheses as to the Society's Political Power-Structure. Of course, for finding out the veracity of these Models, empirical investigations have been conducted by a number of scholars. However, none of these two Models is found to have universal validity. In this context, pioneering investigations conducted by two great scholars may be noted. For instance, Floyd Hunter[19] in his study of the Political Power-Structure of the American city of Atlanta, notices validity of the Monolithic-Pyramidal Model; whereas Robert A. Dahl[20], in his study of the Political Power-Structure of the American City of New Haven, finds empirical evidence in support of the Pluralistic-Polyarchal Model. Thus, no conclusive empirical evidence as to the universal validity of anyone of these two Models is available. Moreover, these empirical investigations have been conducted at the local or community level, and none has yet been undertaken at the State (National) level. Hence, rigorous investigations need to be undertaken at the State-level, and the findings need to be verified again and again in order to make any conclusive statement on the composition of the Society's Political Power-Structure, and also to design an universally valid Model on it.

Notes

1. Robert A. Dahl (1963). *Modern Political Analysis.* New Jersey, USA: Prentice-Hall. Indian Reprint, New Delhi: Prentice-Hall of India, 1972, p. 6.
2. (i) G.E.G. Catlin (1927). *The Science and Methods of Politics.* New York: Knopf. (ii) Frederick M. Watkins (1934). *The State as a Concept of Political Science.* New York: Harper. (iii) Vilfredo Pareto (1935). *The Mind and Society.* New York: Harcourt-Brace. (iv) Gaetano Mosca (1939), *The Ruling Class*: edited by A. Livingston. New York: McGraw Hill. (v) James Burnham (1942). *The Managerial Revolution.* New York: Putman. (vi) Robert Michels, *Political Parties.* Glencoe, Illinois: Free Press, 1942, Originally published in 1915. (vii) Herbert A. Simon (November, 1953). "Notes on the Observation and Measurement of Political Power", *Journal of Politics,* pp. 500-16. (viii) Harold D. Lasswell & Abraham Kaplan (1950). *Power and Society.* New Haven: Yale University Press. (ix) Max Weber (1947). *The Theory of Social and Economic Organization.* Translated by A.M. Handerson & Talcott Parsons. New York: Oxford University Press. (x) Robert A. Dahl. "The Concept of Power", *Behavioural Science, Op. cit,* pp. 201-215. (xi) C. Wright Mills (1969). *Political Elites.* London, George Allen and Unwin Ltd., pp. 67, 112, 120-121, 141. (xii) James G. March (June, 1955). "An Introduction to the Theory and Measurement of Influence", *American Political Science Review,* pp. 431-451.
3. Robert A. Dahl. "The Concept of Power", *Behavioural Science,* pp. 201-215.
4. Robert A. Dahl. *Modern Political Analysis, Op. cit,* p. 32.
5. Geraint Parry (1964). *The Power Elites.* (London, George Allen and Unwin Ltd., 1969), pp. 67, 112, 120-121, and 141.
6. James S. Meisel (1958). *The Myth of the Ruling Class: Gaetano Mosca and the Elite.* Ann Arbor: University of Michigan Press.
7. Geraint Parry. *Political Elites, Op. cit.,* p. 35.
8. Gaetano Mosca. *The Ruling Class, Op. cit.*
9. *Ibid.,* p. 53.
10. Robert Michels. *Political Parties, Op. cit.*
11. *Ibid.,* p. 418.
12. Vilfredo Pareto. *Mind and Society, Op. cit.*
13. James Burnham. *The Managerial Revolution, Op. cit.*
14. C. Wright Mills. *The Power Elites, Op. cit.*
15. Arthur F. Bentley (1908). *The Process of Government.* London: Constable Press.

16. Joseph A. Schumpeter (1976). *Capitalism, Socialism, and Democracy.* London: Allen and Unwin. Originally published in 1942.
17. David Truman (1951). *The Governmental Process.* New York: Alfred A.Knopf.
18. Robert A. Dahl (i) *Who Governs? Op. cit.* (ii) *Polyarchy, Op. cit.* (iii) "A critique of the Ruling Elite Model", *The American Political Science Review,* Vol. 52, June, 1958, pp. 463-69.
19. Floyd Hunter (1963). *Community Power-Structure.* New York, Garden City; Anchor Books.
20. Robert A. Dahl, *Who Governs? Op. cit.*

4

Group Theory of Politics

The Group-Theory presents Groups as the fundamental units of Politics of a Society. Accordingly, it provides a theoretical-construct for the analysis of the Societal Political Process focusing exclusively on group-interactions that involve conflict and co-operation among them in the context of making of authoritative decisions and public policies. Its genesis may be traced to the intellectual contribution of Arthur F. Bentley[1] and subsequently, it has been enriched by the works of a number of scholars among whom David B. Truman[2], Earl Latham[3], Harry Eckstein[4], V.O. Key Jr[5], and L. Herman Zeigler[6] stand out as significant contributors. The basic premise of the Group-Theory of Politics is that Society is composed of a plurality of Groups[7] and hence, it may be structurally portrayed as a mosaic of groups[8] which are of different shapes, sizes, objectives, and dynamics. Its pluralism entails group conflicts which need to be resolved in order to enable the Society to exist, and to continue to exist through time. Thus, Politics understood as the Societal Decision-making Process involves group-conflicts[9], and simultaneously, it becomes concerned with the task of conflict resolution for making and implementing public policies authoritatively so as to enable the Society to maintain and retain its stability and viability. As such, Groups and their interactions constitute the core-area or of Politics of a Society.[10]

The Concept of Group

A Group is defined by Arthur F. Bentley, the founding father of Group-Theory, as "a certain portion of the men of a society taken, however, not as a physical mass cut-off from other masses of men, but as a mass of activity, which does not preclude the men who participate in it from participating likewise in many other group-activities."[11] Following Bentley, the concept of Group is further elaborated by David B. Truman who points out that a Group is a collection of individuals bound together by a common shared attitude, and that the Group "on the basis of one or more shared attitudes makes certain claims upon other groups in the society for the establishment, maintenance, or enhancement of forms of behaviour that are implied by the shared attitudes... The shared attitudes... constitute the interests."[12]

From these conceptualizations, the following defining features or attributes of a Group may be discerned and noted:

1. A Group is constituted of a set of individuals, but it derives its identity from the mass of activities of its members.
2. A Group is formed for attainment and promotion of a common objective or attitude which is shared by its members, and it is this shared attitude which may be termed as its 'interest'. Hence, every group may be termed as an interest group. As pointed out by Arthur F. Bentley, "Group may be well defined in terms of its interest."[13] It is also asserted by David B. Truman who says ". . . interest group refers to any group that on the basis of one or more shared attitudes, make certain claims upon other groups in the society for the establishment, maintenance, or enhancement of forms of behaviour that are implied by the shared attitides."[14]
3. The shared interest of the Group binds its members together, generates cohesion among them, and provides

directions for activities or patterned behaviour of its members for the purpose of effective goal-attainment.

4. The membership of a Group does not preclude or deny its members to associate them and to participate in the activities of other groups. Hence, there emerges the phenomenon of overlapping or cross-cutting membership among the various interest groups in a Society.
5. The activities of all interest-groups create a scenario of group-interactions which involve conflict and co-operation among them for attainment and promotion of their respective interests.

Thus, Groups which are essentially distinct masses of activities constitute a Society both structurally and functionally, and make it dynamic. As Arthur F. Bentley puts it:

> "The great task in the study of any form of social life is the analysis of these groups. When the groups are stated, everything is stated. When I say everything, I mean everything. . . the whole of social life in all its phases can be stated in... groups of active men."[15]

Thus, according to Bentley and other Group-Theorists, Society is composed of a plurality of groups, each with its distinct identity and interest, and each functioning as a mass of activities directed by its own interest for attainment of the cherished goal. The co-existence of these varieties of groups makes the Society a mosaic of Groups. However, since the Groups are different and divergent, their interactions produce a situation of group-conflicts. Of course, their overlapping memberships, and interpretation of interests tend to moderate the group conflicts on inducing them to compromise their respective group-interests. As a consequence, the Society is enabled to maintain its stability and viability.

In the context of societal dynamics produced by group-interactions, there may be discerned some Groups who have explicitly political objectives of capturing political power for making themselves the Government so as to decide, enact, and implement public policies. Such groups may be termed as Political Groups or Political Parties. This distinctive attribute is succinctly focused by a number of distinguished scholars. For instance, according to Joseph A. Schumpeter, the first and the foremost aim of a Political Party " is to prevail over others in order to get into power or to stay in it"[16] according to Joseph LaPalombara and Myron Weiner, the primary objective of a Political Party is "to capture and hold decision making power alone or in coalition with others"[17] and according to Michael Curtis,

> "Essentially party signifies a group of people who hold certain political beliefs in common or who are prepared to support party candidates, work together for electoral victory, attain and maintain political power."[18]

Thus, Political Parties, as Groups of the Society, cherish distinct political objectives, fight at the elections for seeking people's mandate, and form the Government. As distinguished from Political Parties, there are many other groups in the Society which cherish non-political objectives such as social, economic, cultural, and philanthropic objectives etc. without any intention to capture and hold governmental power. These Non-political Groups simply intend to influence the Government and its decision making process for obtaining favourable governmental disposition and policy-decisions so as to attain and promote their respective group-interests. These non-political interest-groups may be termed as 'Pressure Groups.'[19] Thus, their roles, as Harry Eckstein emphatically points out, represent something less than full politicization and something more than utter de-politicization, and constitute "an intermediate level of activity between the political and the apolitical."[20] As such, Society's political or decision-making process, in reality, and in essence, involves the interactions among the Pressure Groups, and also between the Government and the Pressure Groups.

Pressure-Group: Nature and Types

Pressure-Group may be defined, with Harry Eckstein[21], as an organized social group whose members share a common attitude or interest, and which seeks to influence the making of public policies in favour of such attitude or interest without attempting to place its members in formal governmental capacities or offices vitally concerned with its goal, and without even trying to take over any responsibility for the Government for making such authoritative decisions. Thus, it is essentially characterized as a non-partisan organization[22] with a non-political homogenous objective without any intention of seizing the reins of political power and making governmental decisions, but it seeks to influence the Government and its decision-making process for maintenance and enhancement of its cherished goal. This distinctive attribute of a Pressure-Group is also well-emphasized by L. Herman Zeigler when he portrays it as "an organized aggregate which seeks to influence the context of governmental decisions without attempting to place its members in formal governmental capacities."[23]

Pressure-Groups, of course, are of different types and kinds. Following the conceptualization of Gabriel A. Almond and G.B. Powell Jr.[24], these may be broadly classified into four types such as: (i) Anomic-Group, (ii) Non-Associational Group, (iii) Institutional Group, and (iv) Associational Group.

Anomic Group is an organized mass of people without any formal structure, enlisted membership, and defined objectives. It suddenly emerges as and when the grievances of a set of individuals or a section of population remain unheeded and unreleased, for long, by the Government. The dissatisfaction of the aggrieved people gets ventilated through anomic activities involving violence, arson, riots, and assassination etc. against the Government which is identified as the source of frustration and injustice. Since, the unorganized group of people articulate and ventilate their interests and demands through anomic methods, this group is termed as the Anomic-Group. Such groups tend to emerge mostly in under-developed Societies where regular and conventional methods of interest-articulation are either absent or there is an utter failure to address to people's demands and grievances peacefully and constitutionally.

Like Anomic-Group, the Non-Associational Group also lacks in a formal structure but, unlike the Anomic-Group, it does not employ anomic methods of interest-articulation. However, it emerges occasionally basing on the ethnic and cultural identities of people such as their race, caste, gender, language, religion etc., and these groups disband soon after ventilating their demands for attainment of the articulated objectives.

As different from these un-organized groups, the Institutional Group is characterized by a formal structure including an office, enlisted membership, office-bearers, and procedures of action, but it lacks in independence for interest-articulation because it emerges in a formal institution such as the Legislature, the Bureaucracy, the Military, the Political Party etc. in the form of Legislative Blocks, Officers' Club, Military Clique, Party-Wing etc., and hence, it is bound by the rules and regulations of its parent-institution in articulating the interest of its members. Of course, while functioning within the jurisdiction of its parent institution, it tends to exert pressure upon the decision-making authority for the purpose of goal-attainment.

The fourth type of Pressure-Group is the Associational Group which is characterized by normal and befitting attributes for effective interest-articulation and goal-attainment. It is characterized by a formal structure including an office, office-bearers, enlisted membership, procedures of action; and simultaneously, it enjoys freedom for articulating the interest of its members and devising strategies of action for effective goal-attainment on exerting pressure upon the decision-making authority through peaceful, conventional and acceptable methods and techniques. These groups tend to emerge in number and variety mostly in a pluralistic Society where there is a Democratic Polity, and where the values of pluralism and freedom are recognized and practiced in reality. Associational Groups are formed on the basis of different occupations and professions, and may take varieties of names such as, for example, Teachers' Association, Students' Union, Merchants' Association, Chamber of Commerce and Industry, Trade Union, Farmers' Union, Doctors' Association etc. These groups are best suited for undertaking meaningful articulation of interests of their own members, and for effective attainment of their respective group-goals because of their formal structure, on one hand, and the openness of the Political Society, on the other. Moreover, these Groups tend to emerge and grow, in number and variety, compared with other types of Groups, in accordance with the pace and level of development of a Political Society.

Pressure-Group Politics

The term 'Pressure-Group Politics' connotes the roles played by Pressure-Groups in the Political Process of a Society while performing their defined functions. Their functions may be grouped into two major types[25] such as: (i) the Function of Interest-Articulation, and (ii) The Function of Selection of the Relevant Channels of Access for influencing the Government.

Function of Interest-Articulation

The Function of Interest-Articulation is the primary function of a Pressure-Group because it is the shared interest that binds together a set of individuals and motivates them to form the Group. This function may be performed in different styles, what may be termed as modes of expression of demands; and there may be discerned four major pairs of styles[26] such as: (i) Manifest or Latent Style, (ii) Specific or Diffuse Style, (iii) General or Particular Style, and (iv) Instrumental or Affective Style.

A Manifest Style involves an explicit formulation and expression of interest or demand as, for example, a students' union explicitly demands for the provision for greater educational infrastructures in respect of books, journals and teachers; but a Latent Style takes the form of implicit ventilation of demand through behaviour and mood cues as, for instance, simply the display of non-attendance in the classroom or untruly behaviour by the students. A Specific Style involves exact articulation of demand on specifying it precisely and in detail as, for example, a Trade Union makes a demand for fixing the amount of minimum labour-wages with working hours; but a Diffuse Style takes the form of a mere expression of an increase in labour-wages without any detailed specification. A General Style takes the form of articulation of demand for the benefit and advantages of all members of the Group as, for instance, a Merchants' Association makes demand for governmental tax relaxation for all its members; but a Particular Style involves articulation of demand for the advantage of a few of its selected members as, for instance, making a demand for tax-relaxation only for those of its members who have a fixed amount of annual turnover. Finally, an Instrumental Style takes the form of a bargain with consequences realistically spelt out for non-fulfilment of the demand as, for instance, a Caste Group makes a demand for the provision of special status with distinct socio-economic and political privileges, and spells out the consequences of civil disobedience or riots for non-fulfilment of the demand; but an Affective Style involves a simple expression of feelings of gratitude or disappointment respectively in case of fulfilment or non-fulfilment of its demand.

These various Styles seem to characterize the pattern of interest-articulation and mode of expression of demands by a Pressure Group.

Function of Selection of Channels of Access

Soon after a Pressure-Group articulates its interest or demand, it involves itself in the performance of the function of selection of the required Channels of Access in order to reach the Decision-making Centre, and to exert influence upon it for obtaining favourable policy decisions and administrative dispositions. Of course, the Channels of Access are many and varied, but these may be broadly classified into two major categories such as : (i) the Formal Channels of Access, and (ii) the Informal Channels of Access.[27]

Formal Channels of Access

Formal channels of Access are those channels through which a Pressure-Group seeks to reach the Decision-making Centre directly for influencing it. Among the Formal channels of Access, the Mass-media constitute a very useful channel through which the articulated interest of a Pressure-Group may be directly expressed to the Government. Simultaneously, the Mass-media may be used by a Pressure-Group in order to create favourable Public Opinion for its demands, and for influencing the Government. However, the Mass-media may serve as a useful formal channel provided the Polity or the State and its Government permit and encourage freedom of expression and communication, and also, provided these are free from the control of the Elites with vested interests. Besides Mass-media, other important Formal Channels of Access seem to be the Political Parties including the Ruling Party and the Opposition Parties; and the Governmental Institutions such as the Legislature, the Political Executive or Council of Ministers, and the Bureaucracy. A Pressure-Group may communicate its articulated-interest directly through these institutions and their members, and seek to influence the process of decision-making in favour of its interest or demand.

Informal Channels of Access

Informal Channels of Access are those channels through which a Pressure-Group seeks to reach the Decision-making Centre indirectly, and tends to influence it. In this context, Physical Demonstration and Violence constitute an obvious and effective Channel of Access. Physical Demonstration includes a wide variety of techniques and methods such as Strike, Gherao, and Bandh. The method of strike may take different forms such as: (i) General Strike that involves total stoppage of work of all members of a Pressure-Group, (ii) Token Strike that involves stoppage of work of a Pressure-Group in sympathy with the demand of another Pressure-Group, (iii) Work to Rule that involves the performance of routine-work of the office as per rules without displaying special zeal or interest in the office work, (iv) Boycott that involves non-cooperation with the offending employer or decision maker who is also prevented from having any contact with the aggrieved employees, and (v) Picketing that involves prevention of the people from having any contact with the offending employers. As different from Strike, Bandh is a method which is resorted to disrupt the normal life of the common people by way of closing the market, shops, transportation facilities, educational institutions and government offices etc. in order to create inconvenience for them, and thereby, to draw their attention to the unfulfilled demands and to put pressure upon the Government indirectly for fulfilment of the demand. Moreover, a Pressure-Group may resort to the method of Gherao that involves illegal confinement of the offending employer or decision-maker without allowing him to avail physical amenities or needs so as to compel him to agree to its demands. Besides these methods of Physical Demonstration, an aggrieved Pressure-Group may also use the method of Violence that involves commission of Riots entailing destruction of government-property as well as loss of life and property of the people, and even commission of murder or assassination of the offending decision-maker. These different methods of Physical Demonstration and Violence, however, seem to be used by the Pressure-Groups when the conventional and peaceful channels of access are either unavailable or are found to be an utter failure for the purpose of goal-attainment.

Among the conventional and peaceful Informal Channels of Access available to the Pressure-Groups, there may be noted two very useful and effective methods, and these are : (i) Personal Connection, and (ii) Elite-Representation. For influencing the Decision-makers informally, indirectly, but very effectively, a Pressure-Group may seek to establish personal connection with him by way of exploring intimate ties and relationship such as friendship during school and college life, family relationship, ethnic ties, neighbourhood intimacies etc. Establishment of such personal connections with the Decision-maker tends to help a Pressure-Group, to very great extent, for goal-attainment because an approach to a known decision-maker than a stranger would likely to yield favourable decisions.

Apart from 'Personal Connection', another very fruitful informal technique seems to be 'Elite-Representation'. It involves infiltration into the Decision-making Centre incognito, and exploration of a sympathizer through ideological affinity or bribery. A decision-maker who is, thus, made sympathetic to the cause of the Pressure-Group is, most likely, expected to give favourable decisions so that its demands would be effectively realized.

Thus, the Channels of Access are many and varied. Of course, selection of Formal and Informal Channels of Access by a Pressure-Group for reaching the Decision-making Centre, and influencing the Decision-maker tends to be crucially determined by its ability as well as situational convenience to do so.

Determinants of Pressure-Group Politics

Pressure-Group Politics which involves the actual performance of functions of a Pressure-Group in the Political Process of a Society may be analyzed in three broad dimensions such as : (i) Form, (ii) Scope and Intensity, and (iii) Effectiveness.[28] In respect of each of these dimensions, Pressure-Group Politics seems to be determined and conditioned by some major variables or determinants such as the Pattern of Governmental Structure, the Nature of Governmental Policy, and the Attitudinal Pattern of the People. The Pattern of Governmental Structure may be characterized on the basis of the interplay of the decision making power as to whether it is centralized and concentrated or dispersed and distributed. Accordingly, there may be discerned two broad types of Governmental Structure such as the Unitary Governmental Structure, and the Federal Governmental Structure. In the Unitary Governmental Structure, the decision-making power remains centralized in a single National (Central) Government, and that too, in its Executive organ as found, for instance, in the British United Kingdom; whereas, in the Federal Governmental Structure, the decision making power is shared between the Federal Government and the Governments of the Federating States; and even there is distribution of power in each Government among its Legislature, Executive and Judiciary as found, for instance, in the United States of America. For the second variable, as regard the Nature of Governmental Policy, there may be discerned two broad types in view of its social welfare orientation or lack of it. Similarly, as regard the third variable relating to the Attitudinal Pattern of People towards the relevance of group activities, there may be discerned two types such as the Corporatistic Pattern and the Individualistic Pattern. The Corporatistic Attitudinal Pattern emerges when people believe that the Society is essentially composed of groups, not atomistic individuals, and hence, group-activity must be protected and promoted through the political decision-making process. On the contrary, the Individualistic Attitudinal Pattern emerges when people believe that the Society is essentially composed of, not groups, but single atomistic individuals, and hence group-activities may simply be tolerated, not encouraged, in the political decision-making process. On the whole, these three variables, taken together, seem to serve as crucial determinants of Pressure-Group Politics in a Society.

Form of Pressure-Group Politics

By 'Form of Pressure-Group Politics' is meant the Principal Channel of Access which is used by a Group in order to reach the Decision-making Centre, to design a pattern of Relationship with the Government, and to influence it for attainment of the cherished goal. In this context, the Principal Channel of Access to be selected by a Group may be the Formal Channel or the Informal Channel, and also the Pattern of Group-Government Relationship may take the form of Negotiation where the Government duly recognizes the group-demand as decisive, or it may take the form of Consultation where the Government views the group demand non-seriously in making policy-decisions. In a Society where there is Unitary Governmental Structure characterized by centralization and concentration of decision-making power in the Central

Government, and hence, the Decision-making Centre becomes easily identifiable, Pressure-Groups tend to select the Formal Channel as the Principal Channel of Access. Simultaneously, the Pattern of Government-Group Relationship tends to take the form of Negotiation because it enables the governmental representatives to make final decisions on behalf of the Government in the process of their discussions with the group representatives. But, in a Society where there exists Federal Governmental Structure characterized by decentralization and dispersal of decision-making power between the Federal Government and the State Governments, and where there exists distribution of power between the Executive, Legislature, and Judiciary, it may be difficult for the Pressure Groups to locate the final decision-making centre, and hence, they tend to select the Informal Channel as the Principal Channel of Access; and as such, the Pattern of Government-Group Relationship tends to be Consultation.

Simultaneously, the Form of Pressure-Group Politics seems to be determined by the Pattern of Governmental Policy also as to whether it is social-service oriented or not. In case of the welfare or social-service oriented governmental policy which both in its making and implementation require special knowledge and expertise as possessed by a Pressure-Group, the Government recognizes the importance of the concerned groups and hence, the Group is likely to select the Formal Channel as the Principal Channel of Access, and as such, the Pattern of Government-Group Relationship may take the form of Negotiation.

Moreover, the selection of the Principal Channel of Access, and the Pattern of Government-Group Relationship tend to be determined by the Attitudinal Pattern of People as to whether it is corporatistic or individualistic. In case of the Corporatistic Attitudinal Pattern which favours group-activities, Pressure-Groups tend to select the Formal Channel as the Principal Channel of Access; and the Pattern of Government-Group Relationship tends to take the form of Negotiation. But, in case of the Individualistic Attitudinal Pattern which does not encourage group-activities,

Pressure-Groups tend to select the Informal Channel as the Principal Channel of Access, and as such, the Pattern of Government-Group Relationship tends to take the form of Consultation.

Scope and Intensity of Pressure-Group Politics

Scope of Pressure-Group Politics refers to the number and variety of Groups that play their roles in the Political Process of a Society; whereas Intensity refers to the persistence, zeal and favour with which the Groups undertake their activities. In this context, the major determinants seem to be the Pattern of Governmental Structure, the Nature of Governmental Policy, and the Attitudinal Pattern of People. Pressure-Groups tend to emerge and grow in number and variety, and also, they tend to work with persistence and fervour in case of the Unitary Governmental Structure where the final decision-making centre becomes easily located, and where, therefore, the expectation of goal-attainment is brighter; in case of welfare-oriented Governmental Policy that inevitably requires the expertise and cooperation of the Groups in its making and implementation; and in case of the Corporatistic Attitudinal Pattern that favours and encourages group-activities in a Society.

Effectiveness of Pressure-Group Politics

Effectiveness of Pressure-Group Politics refers to the capability and strength of Pressure-Groups for successful goal-attainment while playing their roles in the political process of a Society. In this context, a very significant determinant seems to be a set of attributes of the Group itself. It comprises of the Group's: (i) Physical Resources, (ii) Psychological Resource, (iii) Size, (iv) Organizational Cohesiveness, and (v) Political Skill. Its 'Physical Resources' include: (i) the amount of wealth at its possession, and use of its wealth for popularization of its demands, and for seeking the sympathy of the decision makers; (ii) the ownership of Newspaper or Media-network to create favourable public opinion, and to draw the attention of the Government; and also (iii) the possession of technical skill and expertise that accord it a place of special importance for the decision makers. 'Psychological Resource' refers to the capital of public goodwill and support that it is able to create and harness. Its 'Size' involves the number of members, whether small or large, and also its geographical extensiveness for making its presence felt, and drawing the attention of the Decision-maker. Its 'Organizational-Cohesiveness' refers to the unity and solidarity of the members of the Group, and their genuine commitment to the group-interest. Its 'Political-Skill' connotes the special competence of the group-leaders to devise and employ relevant strategies for influencing the Decision-maker successfully. All these Group attributes, taken together, seem to constitute a vital determinant of effectiveness of a Group in the Political Process of a Society.

Simultaneously, other important determinants such as the Pattern of Governmental Structure, the Nature of Governmental Policy, and the Attitudinal Pattern of People seem to determine the extent of effectiveness of Pressure-Group Politics. Pressure-Groups are likely to play their roles with greater effectiveness in case of the Unitary Governmental Structure where the final decision-making centre is easily located; in case of welfare-oriented Governmental Policy that requires the co-operation of skilled groups in its making and implementation; and in case of the Corporatisic Attitudinal Pattern that favours and encourages group-activities in a Society.

On the whole, Pressure-Group Politics in respect of its Form, Scope and Intensity, and Effectiveness tends to be greatly determined by the Pattern of Governmental Structure, the Nature of Governmental Policy, and the Attitudinal Pattern of People, taken together, in a Society. Additionally, of course, the Attributes of the Groups that compose the Society and play roles in it seem to determine, to a great extent, the Effectiveness of Pressure-Group Politics.

Groups, Government, and Political Stability

Groups perform their roles on articulating the interest of their own members, and on influencing the Government through various channels of access and techniques so as to protect and promote their cherished demands. Group-activities, in this process, create a scenario of inter-group conflicts because of clash of interests. In this conflicting situation, Groups, for realizing their respective articulated interests, as Earl Latham succinctly points out, "combine, break, federate, and form coalitions and constellations"[29], and the socio-political process becomes characterized by "the push and resistance between groups."[30] However, this scenario of inter-group conflicts needs to be resolved for the purpose of maintenance of socio-political stability; and this task is undertaken by the Government on making authoritative decisions and policies. As David H. Truman points out: "Government functions to establish and maintain a measure of order in the relationship among groups."[31] It conducts the process of adjustment of group-activities[32], and plays the role of a mediator or arbiter[33] in the struggle among groups, and seeks to resolve group-conflicts on the basis of the legitimized rules or Constitutional Provisions of the Political Society. In this decision-making process, the task of the Government becomes easier and smoother as the intensity of inter-group conflicts is reduced owing to an unconscious balancing process that prevails among the Groups. This balance of interests among the Groups seems to emerge unconsciously, as David H. Truman points out, due to the phenomenon of overlapping or cross-cutting membership[34] among them. It happens because an individual may become simultaneously a member of various groups such as his caste or tribal group, religious group, language group, gender group, and occupational group etc., and hence, because of overlapping membership in a plurality of groups, there takes place a spontaneous adjustment or balancing of interests among these groups. Consequently, the intensity of inter-group conflicts gets reduced. Moreover, Groups tend to adjust their respective interests with one-another as they perceive it necessary for maintaining and ensuring socio-political stability and order. This perception generates an un-codified, un-written, but widely accepted 'Rule of the Game'[35] or 'habit background'[36] of pursuing group-interests that tends to guide and channelize group-activities, and helps to ensure socio-political order and stability. Consequently, it becomes easier for the Government to address itself to the task of resolution of inter-group conflict, of making and implementing authoritative Public Policies, and of maintaining socio-political order and stability.

A Critical Appraisal

On closer scrutiny, the Group-Theory of Politics seems to contain, within it, some grave lacunae and shortcomings. It completely ignores the role and importance of the individual in the Political Process through which societal decisions and policies are made and implemented. On the contrary, it overemphasizes the role of the Group at the cost of the individual. But, in reality, it is the individual, not the Group, which is the basic unit of the Society. Moreover, a group comes into existence only when like-minded individuals, on sharing a common attitude or interest, form it; and it becomes dynamic only through the activities of its members. How could a group function if each of its members would become indifferent and non-committed to the group goal? Hence, utter neglect of the importance of the individual in the context of the group-dynamics, and also, in the context of the Societal Decision-making Process tends to characterize the Group-Theory as an anti-individualistic, illiberal, and anti-democratic Theory of Politics.

It may also be noted that the Group-Theory fails to reconcile the group-interest with the interest of each one of its members. It focuses on interest-articulation as the primary function of the Group, but it does not ensure that the interest of every member is duly represented when the interest of the Group is decided and articulated. What is the certainty or guarantee that the group-interest represents the interests of all its members, each one taken together, without being the interest of a few dominant members or leaders?

Moreover, the Group-Theory debases the Nature of the Government because it presents the Government as merely an arbiter or reconciliator of group-conflicts in the context of making of Public Policies. Hence, the Government is presented as the societal decision-making institution without an independent will and ability to make public policies, and to govern for the attainment of overall welfare and development of the people as a whole. It is, indeed, a negative perception of the nature of the Government and the State. It reduces Politics merely to an activity of pressure, force, intimidation, and self-interest devoid of public-reason and of peoples' welfare. It also fails to explain why and how systematic changes and development are to be brought about through the political decision-making process of the Society. Thus, this theory smacks of anti-developmentalism.

Group-Theory voices for the maintenance of socio-political equilibrium or stability, but it does not provide any concrete mechanism for its successful attainment. It is also noted that the Group-Theory requires the Government to resolve group-conflicts, and to enact Public Policies for attaining and ensuring socio-political equilibrium or stability. But what is the guarantee that the governmental decisions would be dutifully obeyed by those groups whose interests and demands are ignored and not fulfilled by the Government? How can political stability be maintained and ensured in the event of disobedience and revolt of the dissatisfied and belligerent groups? Moreover, this Theory, on emphasizing on the role of Groups exclusively in the Political Process, fails to provide a coherent conceptual scheme for undertaking a comprehensive study and analysis of the Political Process of a Society because, besides Groups, there are also many other relevant institutions and structures that compose the Political Society, and make it dynamic. Hence, it is an incomplete and partial Theory of Politics for the purpose of socio-political analysis.

However, despite these shortcomings, the Group-Theory signifies a bold academic endeavour for undertaking an empirical and scientific analysis of the Political Process of a Society. It presents a distinct scientific perspective of the Society's Political Process.

Notes

1. Arthur F. Bentley (1908). *The Process of Government: A Study of the Social Pressures.* Chicago: University of Chicago Press.
2. David B. Truman (1951). *The Governmental Process: Political Interests and Public Opinion.* New York: Alfred & Knopf.
3. Earl Latham (1952). *The Group Basis of Politics.* Ithaca, New York: Cornell University Press.
4. Harry Eckstein (1960). *Pressure Group Politics.* Stanford: Stanford University Press.
5. V.O. Key Jr. (1964). *Politics, Parties and Pressure Groups.* New York: T.Y. Crowell.
6. L. Herman Zeigler (1964). *Interest Groups in American Society.* Eaglewood Cliffs., N J.: Prentice Hall.
7. Arthur F. Bentley. *The Process of Government, Op. cit.*, p. 222.
8. David B. Truman. *The Governmental Process, Op. cit.*, p. 32.
9. Charles B. Hagan (1958). "The Group in Political Science", in Ronald Young (ed) (1958). *Approaches to the Study of Politics.* Evanston, Illinois: North Western University Press, 1958, especially, p. 64.
10. Harry Eckstein (1963). "Group Theory and the Comparative Study of Pressure Groups", in Harry Eckstein & David E. Apter (ed): *Comparative Politics: A Reader.* New York: The Free Press of Glencoe, p. 391.
11. Arthur F. Bentley. *The Process of Government, Op. cit.*, p. 211.
12. David B. Truman (1964). *The Governmental Process*, Reprinted. New York: Alfred A. Knopf. pp. 33-34.
13. Arthur F. Bentley. *The Process of Government, Op.cit.*, p. 215.
14. David B. Truman. *The Governmental Process, Op. cit.*, p. 33.
15. Arthur F. Bentley. *The Process of Government, Op. cit.*, pp. 208-09.
16. Joseph A. Schumpeter, *Capitalism, Socialism and Democracy.* Reprinted. London: George Allen and Unwin, 1950, p. 279, 1942 first published.
17. Joseph LaPalombara & Myron Weiner (1966). *Political Parties and Political Development.* Princeton: Princeton University press, p. 6.
18. Michael Curtis (1968). *Comparative Government and Politics.* New York: Harper & Row, p. 37.
19. Harry Eckstein. *Pressure Group Politics, Op.cit.*, pp. 15-39.
20. *Ibid.*, pp. 15-39.
21. *Ibid.*

22. Henry A. Truman (Sept. 1958). "How Pressure Groups Operate" in *the Annals of the American Academy of Political and Social Sciences*, Vol. 319, p. 65.
23. L. Hermon Zeigler. *Interest Groups in American Society, Op. cit.*, p. 30.
24. Gabriel A. Almond and G.B. Powell Jr. (1975). *Comparative Politics—A Developmental Approach*, Boston: Little, Brown and Company, 1966, Indian Reprint, New Delhi: Amerind Publishing Co., pp. 74-79.
25. *Ibid.*, pp. 80-87.
26. *Ibid.*, p. 86.
27. *Ibid.*, p. 80.
28. Harry Eckstein (1960). *Pressure Group Politics*, Stanford: Stanford University Press, pp. 15-39.
29. Earl Latham. *The Group Basis of Politics, Op. cit.*, p. 49.
30. *Ibid.*, p. 49.
31. David H. Truman. *The Governmental Process, Op. cit.*, p. 45.
32. Arthur F. Bentley. *The Process of Government, Op. cit.*, p. 260.
33. (i) Arthur F. Bentley. *The Process of Government, Op. cit.*, Chapter XII, (ii) Earl Latham. *The Group Basis of Politics, Op. cit.*, pp. 33-40.
34. David H. Truman. *The Governmental Process, Op. cit.*, p. 520.
35. *Ibid.*, p. 512.
36. Arthur F. Bentley. *The Process of Government, Op. cit.*, p. 260.

5

Systems Theory of Politics

The Concept of System

The Systems-Theory of Politics is founded on the concept of System which owes its origin to the Science of Biology. The term 'System' seems to have been first coined and used by a Biologist named Ludwig Von Bertanallfy who defines it as "a set of elements standing in interaction."[1] As such, a System is composed of a plurality of elements or objects which cohere together, and tend to influence one another. Yet, the totality of their interactions produces coherence or unity of the System, and gives it an identity quite different and distinguishable from other Systems. Hence, randomly aggregated elements or objects devoid of interrelationships and reciprocal influences among them do not constitute a System. For the emergence of a System, there must be co-existence of a plurality of elements with interaction and interrelationships among them, and each element of the System must contribute, while performing its distinct function, towards the survival and attainment of the systemic-goal. Therefore, a System may be characterized by some distinguishing and universal attributes such as: (i) Comprehensiveness, (ii) Interdependence of Elements, (iii) Existence of a Boundary, (iv) Openness, (v)

Self-Operation, and (vi) Self-Regulation.[2] Its Comprehensiveness connotes the totality of elements that constitute the System and gives it a distinct identity; yet, within the system, each one of its constituting elements retains its own identity in respect of its structure and functions and remains as an inseparable part of the whole System. Simultaneously, all of its constituting elements are interrelated and interdependent with one another in the sense of reciprocal influences, and even, the dysfunction of any-one element tends to affect adversely the functioning of other elements and the performance of the System as a whole. It is this interrelationship among the elements that gives the system a distinct shape, and sets its Boundary or Jurisdiction within which it functions and operates. Its Boundary demarcates the area and space of its operation and also its interaction with other Systems in the total Environment. Therefore, a System is characterized by its Openness because of its tendency for free interactions with other Systems, and it tends to influence the Environment, and in turn, is susceptible to environmental influences. In this context, environmental influences constitute INPUTS for the System, whereas the System's endeavours to influence the Environment constitute its OUTPUTS. This constant interaction between the System and its Environment makes the System a dynamic entity on enabling it to function as a 'Self-Operating Input-Output Apparatus'. Simultaneously, the System on receiving negative feedback information from the Environment on its performance tends to regulate or change itself suitably for its survival, and, thus, it works as a 'Self-Regulating Mechanism' or entity.

This concept of a System with its universal attributes seems to have greatly influenced intellectual endeavours of Modern Political Scientists in designing the System-Theory of Politics for the purpose of understanding and analyzing Politics and Political Phenomena of a Society in systemic-perspective. In this context, however, there may be noted two significant, yet different theoretical Models such as: (i) the Systemic-Persistence Model conceptualized by David

Easton[3], and (ii) the Systemic-Maintenance Model conceptualized by Gabriel A. Almond.[4]

Easton's Systemic-Persistence Model

The Systemic-Persistence Model is the intellectual construct of David Easton. It is designed on the basis of his concept of Political System which he defines as "a set of interactions abstracted from the totality of social behaviour through which values are authoritatively allocated for a society."[5] The Political System is, thus, conceptualized as a System of people's behaviour or activities relating specifically to Societal Politics that encompasses the entire process of authoritative allocation of societal values, in all of its dimensions, involving the formation of demands on the basis of people's values or preferences on societal issues, the transmission of these demands to the Authority or Government of the Society, and the enactment and implementation of public policies legitimately. As a System of Politics, it is simultaneously characterized by the universal systemic attributes of comprehensiveness, interdependence of parts or elements, existence of a boundary, openness, self-operation, and self-regulation; and also, it functions as an Input-Output Political Apparatus for allocating people's values authoritatively. However, in the process of discharging its functions, its prime-concern or ultimate-goal that it seeks to attain is "Systemic-Persistence". According to Easton, 'Systemic-Persistence'[6] connotes retention and attainment of two life-conditions[7] or essential variables of the Political System such as: (i) its ability to allocate values for the Society, and (ii) its ability to get these allocations accepted as authoritative by most of its people through time. These life-conditions constitute the core of Easton's definition of the Political System, and are, also, explicit in it. According to him, every Political System, while performing its functions, strives always to retain and fulfil these two life-conditions, and tends to persist through time. In this context, the dynamics of the Political System as a Political Input-Output Apparatus striving always for attainment of the ultimate goal of systemic-persistence is explained by Easton through a diagram illustrated below:

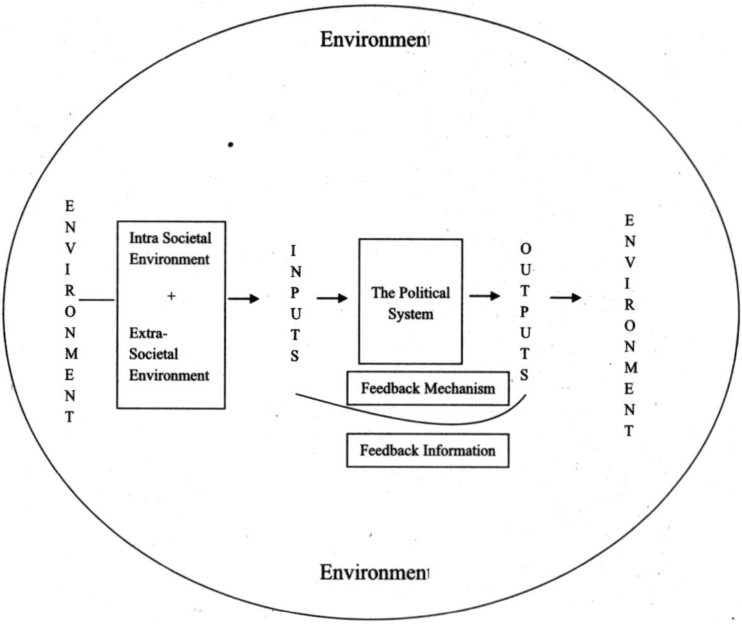

A Diagram of Easton's Model of Political System[8]

The Political System of a Society exists and operates in a Comprehensive Environment, which is composed of both the Intra-Societal Environment and the Extra-Societal Environment.[9] The Intra-Societal Environment includes all internal domestic Systems of the Society such as its Ecological System, Biological System, Demographic System, Social System, Cultural System, Economic System etc.; whereas the Extra-Societal Environment includes all Systems of the International Society such as the International Political System, International Demographic System, International Ecological System, International Social System, International Economic System etc. All these Systems of the International Society along with all these Systems of the National Society constitute the total Environment within which the Political System exists, operates, and interacts. The constant interaction between the

Political System and the Environment manifests the process in which the Political System is influenced by the Environment through Inputs, and simultaneously, the Political System tends to influence the Environment through Outputs. The Inputs consist of people's Demands and Support, combined together, relating to varieties of societal issues. In this context, Demand connotes "an expression of the opinion that authoritative allocation with regard to a particular subject matter should or should not be made by those responsible for doing so."[10] In this process of formation of Demand, both the Intra-Societal Environment and the Extra-Societal Environment tend to play key and crucial roles. For instance, inflation which is essentially an issue of the Domestic Economic System may influence and motivate people to make Demand upon the Political System for enactment of suitable laws and policies for controlling and stabilizing the prices of essential goods and commodities. Similarly, war which is essentially an issue of the International Political System may influence and motivate the people to make Demand upon the National Political System for enactment of policies as deemed necessary for ensuring national safety and security. Thus, the people of a Society may make demands upon their Political System for enactment of authoritative public policies because of the impact and influence of the Intra-societal Environment as well as the Extra Societal Environment. However, these Demands made by the people on varieties of societal issues need to be coupled with their support for constituting Inputs. In this context, 'Support' which is an integral part of the Input may be defined as favourable orientation and behaviour of the people towards the Political System.[11] Support may be of two types[12] such as: (i) Covert Support which takes the form of favourable feelings, sentiments, and attitudes, and (ii) Overt Support which takes the form of favourable activities and behaviour. These two types of Support are interrelated because overt support emanates from covert support, which, in turn, is founded on people's legitimacy towards the Political System and its structural components. Thus, when Support of the people towards the Political System becomes combined with their Demands on varieties of societal issues, Inputs are formed, and are fed into the Political System for making of authoritative decisions or Outputs. As a consequence, the Political System becomes enlivened and dynamic.

Dynamics of the Political System

The Political System as an apparatus for undertaking authoritative allocation of values for the Society becomes dynamic when its structural components become active and energized. According to Easton, the Political System comprises of three major Structural Objects or components[13], and these are: (i) the Political Community, (ii) the Regime, and (iii) the Authority. In this context, 'the Political Community'[14] refers to the total body of members of the Political System considered as a coherent group of persons bound together by a common political division of labour for attainment common political objectives through a common structure and set of processes; 'the Regime'[15] connotes the Constitutional Order including Values (goals), Norms (Principles and Procedures), and Structure of Authority (the pattern of distribution of legitimate power) that provide the framework for political interactions and making of authoritative decisions; and 'the Authority'[16], refers to the set of persons who are incumbents or occupants of the Authoritative Decision-Making Structure including the Legislature, the Executive, and the Judiciary. These structural components or objects are also the Objects of Support that need people's legitimacy for becoming active and energized so as to discharge the prime-task of making and implementing authoritative decisions and policies. Simultaneously, people's support towards these Structural Objects or Components of the Political System facilitates the process of formation of Inputs. Thus, people's Support towards the Political System on being combined with their Demands on varieties of societal issues form the Inputs.[17] These Inputs which take shape as a consequence of the influences of the total Environment upon the members of the Political Community are fed into the Political System to be processed into Outputs. In this process of production of Outputs or authoritative Public Policies, the incoming Inputs are subjected to scrutiny by the Authority for finding out their compatibility with the Regime or Constitutional Order. Thus, the Legislature, as part of the Authority, produces Outputs by way of enacting laws and public policies in responding to the Inputs; the Executive, as a part of the Authority, implements these Outputs authoritatively; and the Judiciary, as a part of the Authority, adjudicates the Outputs for ensuring again their conformity with the Constitutional Order. These Outputs are, thus, made and implemented by the Political System in the context of discharging its prime task of authoritative allocation of values for the Society. The authoritative implementation of Outputs, however, may generate people's reactions, either positive or negative, towards the Political System; and these reactions and opinions may be termed as Feedback Information because these are transmitted back and fed into the Political System in the form of Secondary Input for production of Outputs by the Authorities. Moreover, the Authorities may also make Demands upon the Political System, and help-form Inputs which may be termed as 'Withinputs'. All these types of Inputs such as Original Inputs, Secondary Inputs, and Withinputs are processed by the Political System for production of Outputs or authoritative public policies. Simultaneously, the Political System tends to respond to these feedback information and opinions of the people in the context of its dynamics for attainment of the ultimate goal of systemic-persistence. Of course, the feedback information tends to be of crucial importance for attainment of the goal of systematic-persistence specifically in the event of formation of Negative Feedback Information that contains people's dissatisfaction towards the Outputs produced by the Political System. Such dissatisfaction, if remains unheeded and unsolved by the Political system, may ultimately entail people's withdrawal of support and legitimacy, and may pave for political instability, disintegration, and non-attainment of the goal of systemic-persistence. Hence, the Political System is required to be attentive and alert to the Negative Feedback Information that comes to it from the Environment.

Thus, Easton conceptualizes 'A Dynamic Response Model'[18] of the Political System, and presents that the Political System is in a state of constant and regular interactions with the Environment in the sense that the Environment tends to influence the Political System on facilitating the formation of Inputs, and that the Political System tends to influence the Environment through Outputs produced by it. These interactions, indeed, enliven the Political System, and make it a dynamic political apparatus engaged in the task of authoritative allocation of values for the Society. However, systemic-dynamics may be seriously challenged, and the attainment of the goal of systemic-persistence may be seriously impeded by these environmental interactions that may create challenges for the Political System, and may incapacitate it to retain its life conditions. These challenges to the Political System may be termed as 'Systemic-Stresses'.[19]

Systemic-Stresses

The Political System may experience and encounter Stresses in the context of its dynamics because of its openness and its continuous interactions with the Environment where Inputs consisting of Demands and Support originate and take shape. Since Stresses are caused by detrimental Inputs, there may be discerned two major types of Stresses such as: (i) Demand-Stress[20], and (ii) Support-Stress.[21] Demand-Stress emerges when Demands, in respect of their quantity and substance, tend to endanger the allocative ability of the Political System to produce authoritative outputs or decisions. As such, it includes both Volume-Stress[22] and Content-Stress.[23] It may be termed as Volume-Stress if the Political System experiences serious difficulties to produce authoritative outputs, within a specified time-limit, due to quantitative excess or over-load of a huge number of Demands made by the people upon it. On the contrary, it may be termed as Content-Stress if the Political System experiences inability to process the incoming Demands into authoritative decisions or Outputs due to their qualitative excess in the sense of their incompatibility with the normative framework and constitutional order of the Political System.

Besides these types of Demand-Stresses, the Political System may also experience Support-Stress which may emerge in relation to the 'Support' component of the Input. It involves serious difficulties experienced by the Political System in processing the incoming Inputs because of loss, decline, or erosion of support of the people, below a minimal level, towards each of its three structural components or objects such as the Political Community, the Regime, and the Authority. Support-Stress may emerge in the event of occurrence of widespread and irreconcilable differences and disagreement among the people on the common pattern of basic political values and norms that constitute the foundation of the Political Community. For instance, if the Political Community is founded on the basic values of Democracy or Communism but subsequently different sections of the population cherish and champion such political values which are inconsistent and antagonistic to its foundational values, the consequence may be emergence of Support-Stress that would destabilize, and even disintegrate the Political System. Support-Stress may also emerge at the level of the Regime if different sections of the population would refuse to respect and obey the Constitutional Order. Similarly, the Political System, at the level of its Authority, may experience Support-Stress when most of its people refuse to obey the decisions of the incumbents of the Authority, and consequently, it would be unable to implement and enforce its authoritative decisions effectively. As such, on the whole, the Political System may experience Support-Stress in the sense of loss, decline, or erosion of support of the people relating to the Political Community, the Regime, and the Authority which taken together constitute the Structure[24] of the Political System.

Thus, various types of Demand-Stress and Support-Stress may create serious difficulties for the Political System to attain and realize its ultimate goal of Systemic-Persistence as and when the Inputs that come into the Political System in the combined form of Demand and Support endanger its ability to allocate values, and to enforce its decisions authoritatively. Demand-Stress tends to endanger the allocative ability of the Political System, whereas Support-Stress tends to endanger its ability to implement decisions and policies authoritatively. When these stressful experiences become intolerable and unmanageable by the Political System, and its essential variables or life-conditions are seriously endangered, the Political System may find itself at the vicinity of its entropy or death. Such a stressful condition is termed as "Critical Range"[25]—a condition in which the collapse or disintegration of the Political System is imminent. However, according to Easton, there is a natural propensity of the Political System to strive to survive and persist, and hence it tends to regulate and reduce the varieties of Stresses, to keep these within the tolerable and manageable limit, and to avoid its entry into the Critical Range by way of taking the help of some Stress-Regulation Mechanisms.

Stress-Regulation Mechanisms and Systemic-Persistence

For regulation of Demand-Stress including Volume-Stress and Content-Stress, the Political System may utilize the services of some important Stress-Regulation Mechanisms[26] such as Structural Mechanism, Cultural Mechanism, Communication Mechanism, and Reduction Mechanism.

Structural Mechanisms include such institutions or structures as Pressure Groups, Political Parties, Mass-media, Formal Groups, and Informal Groups of Opinion Leaders and Elites who help-form people's demands, in terms of both quantity and quality, on varieties of societal issues for the purpose of political processing. These structures work as Gate-keepers, and may protect the Political System from the adverse-affects of Demand-Stress by way of regulating the quality and quantity of Demands in favour of the Political System. Besides the Structural Mechanisms, there are also varieties of socio-cultural groups such as family, racial and ethnic groups, religious groups, and occupational groups etc.

which work as Cultural Mechanisms; and these may help-reduce Demand-Stress on socializing the people in the values of peaceful co-existence, co-operation and national integration. Demand-Stress may also be reduced through the working of the Mass-media such as Newspapers, Radio, Television, Journals, and Magazines etc. which transmit and disseminate system-allegiant information and values to the people. Moreover, in the context of Demand-Stress Regulation, favourable and conducive role may be played by the Reduction Mechanisms which include institutions such as Pressure Groups, Political Parties, and the Legislature that help-reduce demand-overload by way of combining compatible demands, and reducing them to a limited number of compact policy-proposals before these are taken up for decision-making and production of public policies.

For regulating and reducing Support-Stress, the Political System may devise and use various measures for creating in the people a high sense of generalized attachment, at the minimum, what Easton terms as Diffuse-Support[27], towards the entire Political System including its structural components or objects such as the Political Community, the Regime, and the Authority. Diffuse-Support constitutes a "Reservoir of favourable attitude or goodwill"[28] of the people; and it is unconditional and without any expectation of direct or specific benefits, and it motivates the people even "to accept or tolerate outputs... which they see as damaging to their wants."[29] It is, therefore, akin to a sense of patriotism or nationalism of the people; and it helps-create in them an allegiant psychology that issues forth in supportive behaviour, and enables the Political System to persist through time. For creating it in the people, the Political System may take the help of various agents and agencies, both non-political and political, such as Family, School and Educational Institutions, Peer Groups and other Socio-Cultural Groups, Mass-media, Political Parties etc. that play significant roles in the process of political socialization.[30] Apart from undertaking endeavours for generating generalized support in the people towards it, the Political System may also work and strive to obtain specific support of the people by way of providing Outputs or Policies in satisfaction to people's demands and desires, and if necessary, on changing the Outputs in conformity with the Negative Feedback Information so as to keep the people satisfied and allegiant.[31]

Thus, the Political System tends to regulate and reduce both Demand-Stress and Support-Stress experienced by it through the help of various Stress-Regulation Mechanisms, and also on devising both long-term and short-term measures and strategies. As such, it strives to avoid its entropy including its collapse and disintegration, and simultaneously, to attain and realize the ultimate goal of Systemic-Persistence that requires retention of its ability to allocate values (Demands), and to get these allocations accepted as legitimate and authoritative by the people through time. However, in the process of attainment of the prime-goal of Systemic-Persistence, the Political System may change itself frequently and radically in respect of its Form (overall Structure) and Norms (Political Culture), if so required, but it must retain the two life-conditions pertaining to its ability to undertake the task of making authoritative allocation of values for the Society, and implementing these decisions effectively.

Almond's Systemic-Maintenance Model

The Systemic-Maintenance Model is designed by Gabriel A. Almond on the foundation of his concept of Political System. He defines the Political System as "that system of interactions to be found in all independent societies which performs the functions of integration and adaptation (both internally vis-à-vis other societies) by means of the employment, or threat of employment, of more or less legitimate physical compulsion."[32] Almond, like Easton, views political life of every Society in systemic-perspective, but unlike Easton, presents the central concern of the Political System as "maintenance of its basic structure and culture" through time. According to him, the Political System of a Society, structurally, is a System of people's behaviour and interactions in relation to Politics which is essentially characterized by legitimate physical compulsion or power in making and implementing authoritative decisions and policies. At the same time, functionally, it always tends, and strive to maintain and keep its Structure (Form) integrated, and the congruent (supporting) Political Culture intact, through time by way of adapting to, or adjusting with, the environmental influences and challenges. As such, the prime-goal of the Political System is 'Systemic-Maintenance' which it seeks to attain, in the process of its dynamics, on maintaining its Structure and the congruent Political Culture intact, and that too, with no vital change in them, by way of using its legitimate power if it is so needed. The dynamics of the Political System is explained by Almond through a diagram as illustrated below.

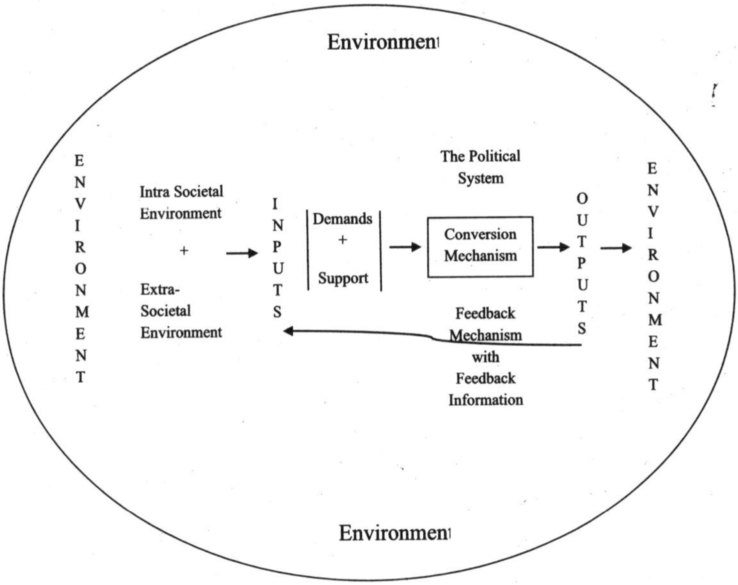

The Systemic-Maintenance Model[33] of the Political System

The Political System, according to Almond, is characterized by the universal systemic-attributes such as Comprehensiveness, Independence of Parts or Elements, Existence of a Boundary, Openness, Self-Operation, and Self-Regulation. It exists and operates in a broad Environment which is composed of both the Intra-Societal Environment (the National Society) and the Extra-Societal Environment (the Inter-national Society). As an integral part of the total Environment, the Political System is susceptible to the environmental influence which come to it in the form of Inputs that consist of Demands of the people on varieties of societal issues and their Support towards the Political System. People's Demands are classified by Almond into four broad[34] categories such as : (i) Demands for allocation of goods and services as, for instance, demands for wages and salaries, educational opportunities, health services, employment in public services etc., (ii) Demands for regulation of behaviour as, for instance, demands for provisions for safety and security of life and property, control over market and prices of the commodities etc., (iii) Demands for participation in the Political System as, for instance, demands for the right to vote, to contest at the elections, to hold public offices, to organize political associations and parties etc., and (iv) Demand for communication and information as, for instance, demands for owning and operating media of communications, for the right to be informed of governmental decisions and policies etc. All these varieties of Demands may be combined in various forms and degrees of intensity.

Apart from Demand, the other component of the Input is Support which may be classified, according to Almond, into four major types[35] such as : (i) Material Support as, for instance, payment of taxes and other levies, undertaking of public services, both civil and military etc., (ii) Behavioural Support as, for instance, obedience to laws and regulations, maintenance of public order and peace, (iii) Participatory Support as, for instance, voting at the elections, participation in political activities in support of the Political System, and (iv) Moral Support as, for instance, payment of respect to public authorities, symbols and ceremonials of the Political System with a high sense of patriotism and nationalism. All these various types of Support may be combined with various kinds of Demands in variety of ways, and accordingly, Inputs are formed. These Inputs which originate in the Environment owing to the environmental influences are fed into the Political System, and are processed by its Conversion Mechanism with reference to the constitutional provisions. As a consequence, Outputs (Authoritative Decisions and Policies) are produced. These Outputs, according to Almond, may also be classified into four broad categories[36], such as : (i) Extractive Outputs as, for instance, taxes and levies to be paid by the people, and services to be undertaken for public offices, both civil and military; (ii) Regulative Outputs as, for instance, laws and regulations enacted for regulating people's behaviour for purpose of maintaining public order and national security; (iii) Distributive Outputs as, for instance, public policies enacted for people's material welfare and well-being; and (iv) Symbolic Outputs as, for instance, laws and regulations enacted for honouring national symbols and holding national ceremonies etc.

Thus, the Political System works as an Open System on responding to varieties of Inputs; as a Self-Operating System on processing the incoming Inputs into varieties of Outputs with the help of its conversion mechanism; and also, as a Self-Regulating System by way of changing its Outputs provided such changes do not challenge and hinder, but promote the attainment of the ultimate goal of Systemic-Maintenance. As such, the Political System functions as an Input-Output Political Apparatus that produces Outputs in response to the Inputs as deemed necessary for effective attainment of the prime-goal of Systemic-Maintenance. The dynamics of the Political System, of course, involves performance of some major types of functions.

Functions of the Political System

The Political System, according to Almond, becomes dynamic with the performance of two major types universal systemic-functions such as: (i) the Conversion Function[37], and the System-Maintenance and Adaptation Function.[38]

The Conversion Function is the most fundamental function of the Political System as its performance makes it to work as a self-steering system which is, therefore, enabled to process and convert Inputs into Outputs. It involves performance of six sub-types of functions[39], such as: (i) Interest-Articulation Function, (ii) Interest-Aggregation Function, (iii) Rule-Making Function, (iv) Rule-Application Function, (v) Rule-Adjudication Function, and (vi) Political Communication Function. The function of Interest-Articulation is the first functional step that initiates the System's conversion process because it involves the task of formation of interests (Demands) of various sections people on issues that pertain to them. This function of Interest-Articulation is followed by the performance of the function of Interest-Aggregation that involves making of alternative policy-proposals on aggregating (combining) compatible articulated interests of various groups of people. It, thus, facilitates the formation of Inputs consisting of Demands of the people on varieties of societal issues and their Support towards the Political System. The Inputs, thus formed, are fed into the Political System for the purpose of conversion into Outputs (Authoritative Decisions and Public Policies). This process of conversion of Inputs into Outputs involves performance of three functions such as the Rule-Making Function, the Rule-Application Function, and the Rule-Adjudication Function. In this process, the incoming Inputs are subjected to scrutiny on referring to the norms and provisions of the constitution; and the acceptable Inputs are made the basis of enactment of laws, rules, regulations, and public policies. This Rule-Making Function is followed by the performance of the Rule-Application Function that involves implementation of the enacted laws and public policies. It is followed by the performance of the Rule-Adjudication Function as and when there would emerge the need for scrutiny and review of the laws for ascertaining their constitutionality. The performance of this Rule-Adjudication Function enables the Political System to work as a Self-Regulating System on correcting its errors in conformity with the adjudicated constitutional provisions.

Of course, the performance of each of these sub-types of Conversion Functions inevitably necessitates the performance of the

Political-Communication Function which involves transmission and dissemination of explicitly political information as well as politically relevant non-political information in the entire process of conversion of Inputs into Outputs. As such, the performance of the Political-Communication Function greatly facilitates the performance of the Interest-Articulation Function and the Interest-Aggregation Function which are concerned with the formation of Inputs, and simultaneously, it immensely facilitates the performance of the Rule-Making Function, the Rule-Application Function, and the Role-Adjudication Function which are concerned with the formation of the Outputs and their implementation. Therefore, unless the Political-Communication Function is performed, neither Inputs may be made nor processed into Outputs, and consequently, the Political System may become defunct.

In the context of the dynamics of the Political System, the second major type of function that is performed is the Function of System-Maintenance and Adaptation which is termed by Almond as the Function Political Socialization and Recruitment.[40] The Political Socialization Function involves the induction of people into that pattern of Political Culture which is congruent with, and supportive to the overall Structure (Form) of the Political System. The successful performance of this function is essential for the survival of the Political System by way of maintaining its Structure and Culture intact. In this context, Political Culture which connotes the pattern of people's orientations towards the Political System needs to be allegiant so that the Structure-Culture Congruent Relationship would enable it to maintain itself effectively, and to remain stable and viable through time. Simultaneously, the Political System, in order to maintain itself, is required to perform the Function of Political Recruitment that involves selection and appointment of personnel for the performance of all its different types of systemic-functions and system-related functions which are necessary for making it dynamic as well as for maintaining its Structure and Culture.

Thus, according to Almond, every Political System is characterized by the phenomenon of universality of political functions[41] in the sense that it performs all seven major types of functions such as the functions of Interest-Articulation, Interest-Aggregation, Rule-Making, Rule-Application, Rule-Adjudication, Political Communication, and Political Socialization and Recruitment. However, since the Political System is envisioned as an Input-Output Political Apparatus, these functions may be broadly categorized as Input Functions and Output Functions. In this context, the Input Functions include the Functions of Interest-Articulation, Interest-Aggregation, Political Communication, and Political Socialization and Recruitment; whereas the Output Functions include the Functions of Rule-Making, Rule-Application, and Rule-Adjudication. As and when the Input Functions are performed, there takes place formation of Inputs and their transmission into the Political System; whereas the performance of the Output Functions entails production of Outputs and their implementation.

Consequently, the Political System becomes dynamic, and strives to attain the ultimate goal of Systemic-Maintenance. Of Course, every Political System tends to perform these functions through some institutions or structures which may be specific or diffuse (multi-functional), and hence, it is characterized by the phenomenon of universality and multi-functionality of structures.[42] As such, there is formed a distinct pattern of Function-Structure Relationship that tends to influence the dynamics of the Political System.

Functional-Structural Relationship

According to Almond, ideally, the seven major types of functions of the Political System need to be performed by distinct types of structures. He postulates that the Functions of Political Socialization and Recruitment, Political-Communication, Interest-Articulation, Interest-Aggregation, Rule-Making, Rule-Application and Rule-Adjudication need to be performed by distinct, specific, and corresponding Structures such as Political-Socializers and Recruitment Agencies, Mass-media, Pressure-Groups, Political Parties, Legislature, Executive and Judiciary respectively. Thus, for the performance of each Function, Almond identifies and assigns a distinct, specific, and corresponding Structure. This pattern of Functional-Structural Relationship[43] is, thus, characterized by the Principles of Structural-Differentiation, and the Principle of Functional Specialization and Specificity.[44] As such, Almond's Functional Theory of the Polity that presents the Model of a Developed Political System requires its, all political and quasi-political functions to be different from one another, and be performed with increasing specialization by specific, and distinct structures. These structures, also, need to be different from one another. Hence, even though every Political System is characterized by the Principles of Universality of Functions and Universality of Structures, the level of its development tends to be conditioned and shaped in conformity with the degree of its structural differentiation, and functional specificity-cum specialization. It also tends to shape the pattern of the Political System's Systemic-Capability.

Systemic-Capability

According to Almond, the Political System's 'Systemic-Capability' connotes is "over-all performance as a distinct unit in the environment."[45] It involves the total dynamics of the Political System, and it may be discerned and classified into four broad categories[46] such as: (i) Extractive Capability, (ii) Regulative Capability, (iii) Distributive capability, and (iv) Responsive Capability. All these types of capabilities relate to the Outputs produced by the Political System in processing Inputs into Outputs. In this context, the Extractive Capability may be characterized on the basis of the extent and range of human and material resources which the Political System is able to draw from the people in the form of taxes and services. The Regulative Capability may be characterized on the basis of the scope of the Political System and its ability to regulate and control people's behaviour as deemed necessary for maintenance of socio-political order and stability. The distributive capability may be characterized on the basis of the scope and range of the Political System and its ability to allocate and distribute goods and services for the benefit and welfare of the people through public-policy measures. The Responsive Capability may be characterized on the basis of the System's tendency to remain responsible to the people and responsive to public-opinion sincerely.

All these types of Systemic Capability, according to Almond, tend to determine the overall performance of the Political System as a distinct unit in the Environment in the context of flow of Inputs into it, and production of Outputs by it. However, the Political System is required to use and adjust its capabilities in such a way as to attain the ultimate goal of Systemic-Maintenance through time. In this context, of course, its Responsive Capability[47] seems to be of great significance because it tends to enable the Political System immensely to obtain people's legitimacy and spontaneous support. If the people believe in the goodness of the Political System and its people-friendly governance, they tend to legitimize it. Therefore, the Responsive Capability tends to form in the people a high sense of belongingness to the Political System; and consequently, people are motivated to pay taxes and render services spontaneously, and also to abide by its laws and rules willingly. As such, on acquiring people's supportive behaviour, the Political System is enabled to have greater Extractive Capability and Regulative Capability. Simultaneously, its greater Extractive Capability enables it to have greater Distributive Capability for allocating and distributing its material resources for the welfare of the people. Hence, display of greater Responsive Capability seems to be the foundation of greater overall Systemic Capability of the Political System, and as such, the Political System becomes enabled to acquire and attain a greater status in the context of its modernization and development.[48]

Political System, Political Culture, and Political Development

Almond's Systemic-Maintenance Model of Political System is essentially designed for attainment of Political Development.

According to him, Political Development may be attained provided the Political System remains durably stable. Of course, stability may be attained provided the Political System maintains its Structure (Form) and the Congruent Political Culture intact for long. Hence, Structure-Culture Congruent Relationship is an essential condition for attainment of political stability. However, political stability, for long, may be obtained provided the Political System possesses and displays high Responsive Capability because 'Will, not force is basis of the State', and the 'Will' to obey tends to be generated from a sense of belongingness to the Political System. As such, the Responsive Capability of the Political System motivates the people to render spontaneous, and willing obedience to it, and it also helps-form higher overall Systemic-Capability which, in turn, tends to enable it to function as a great and strong Nation-State. Thus, high Responsive Capability seems to make the Political System, both structurally and functionally, a strong and vibrant Democratic Polity. Of Course, the Structure of the Democratic Polity needs to be maintained intact on being supported by the Civic Culture[49] which is a distinct Pattern of Allegiantly Participant Secular Political Culture that tends to make the people rational, national, secular, and empirical in their orientation and behaviour. Moreover, the Civic Culture that makes the people rational and pragmatic in their orientations and behaviour tends to help-form greater structural-differentiation and functional specificity-cum specialization in the context of Functional-Structural Relationship of the Political System.

As such, formation of the Civic Culture[50] in the people seems to be an essential condition for attainment of the ultimate political goal of Systemic-Maintenance with Political Development as it tends to enable the Political System to have greater Systemic-Capability, and greater Structural Differentiation-cum-Functional Specialization. Thus, it is the Pattern of Political Culture that tends to determine the level of Political Development of a Political System.

A Critical Appraisal

Both the Systemic-Persistence Model of Easton and the Systemic-Maintenance Model of Almond are grand Models of Political Life conceptualized and designed for the purpose of empirical analysis of Politics of a Society scientifically and comprehensively. However, on closer scrutiny, each one seems to be incomplete in the sense of being partially realistic. The Systemic-Persistence Model focuses exclusively on attainment of the ultimate goal of persistence or survival of a Political System and requires it to undertake endeavours for constantly retaining its ability to allocate values and simultaneously, to get these allocations accepted as legitimate and binding by its people through time. In the process of its endeavour to retain the two essential variables or life-conditions, Easton's Model remains unconcerned for the need of retention of its prevalent Structure (Form) and the Congruent Political Culture; rather it allows the Political System to change and modify them, frequently and even radically, if it is so deemed necessary. Even though frequent and radical changes are brought about in the Structure and its Political Culture, the Political System, according to Easton, does not die but persists as long as it is able to allocate, and enforce its decisions authoritatively. However, this provision for allowing vital changes in the Structure and Political Culture of the Political System frequently and radically would, most likely, entail political and governmental instability. Hence, Easton's Model seems to generate and foster, in real world situations, socio-political chaos, disorder, and instability.

Similarly, the Systemic-Maintenance Model of Almond, on closer scrutiny, seems to be an incomplete and partially realistic model. It focuses exclusively on the attainment of the ultimate-goal of Systemic-Maintenance by way of keeping and retaining the prevalent Structure and its Congruent Political Culture intact through-time, and it does not allow vital changes to be made in them. Its premise is that vital changes in the Political System's Structure (Form) and Culture, if these are made, would entail entropy or death of the prevalent Political System, and consequently, there would emerge a new Political System with a new structure and political culture. As such, this Model of Almond seems to be unconcerned with the need and also the desirability of political changes. In real world situations, change is the law of life, and hence, no Society can prevent and deny changes in its socio-political life and order. Hence, every Political System must change from time to time in conformity with the people's will and opinion born out of changes in the socio-economic and political environment. Thus, Almond's Model seems to be a status-quoist and static model of political life. Moreover, this Model seems to be culture-bound in the sense that the theory of Function-Structure Relationship, and the theory of Systemic-Capability are supportive of democratic values and principles as against the communist, authoritarian, and non-western political ideologies.

Thus, both the Model of Easton and the Model of Almond seems to contain some unrealistic premises. Yet, their importance and relevance must not be ignored in the realm of scientific and comprehensive analysis of Political Life of a Society. The primary lacunae and shortcoming of both these two Models may be obviated and remedied if the systemic-persistence perspective and the systemic-maintenance perspective are synthesized and combined together in view of the reality of socio-political existence. In the real-world situations, political stability is as needed as political change. Every Political System, howsoever stable and viable it is, cannot remain indifferent to the demands and the need for political changes because its very survival requires it to change in response to changes in the socio-economic and political environment and the emerging demands of the people so that it would obtain peoples' support and legitimacy, and would, consequently, remain stable. Similarly, no Political System can ignore and remain indifferent to the need for socio-political stability because, lacking in stability and effective maintenance of itself, it may lapse into socio-political chaos and disorder that would, ultimately, pave for its entropy and disintegration. Hence, the need for political stability is as important as the need for orderly change. As such, neither the Systemic-

Maintenance Model nor the Systemic-Persistence Model provides a completely realistic perspective; each one is found to be partially realistic and hence, incomplete in itself.

Therefore, in view of the reality of political life and existence, both these Models need to be synthesized and combined because of the utter need for political stability and of the inevitability of political changes in the political process of every Political System so that fruitful and meaningful empirical analysis of Politics of a Society may be undertaken.

Notes

1. Ludwing Von Bertanallfy (1968). "General System Theory" in *General Systems*, Vol. I, (1956), p. 3 cited in Oran R. Young (ed): *Systems of Political Science*. Englewood Cliff, N. J., Prentice-Princeton Hall, Inc, p. 15.
2. (i) David Easton (1965). *A Framework for Political Analysis*. Englewood Cliffs, N. J. Prentice Hall, Inc., p. 24, and *A Systems Analysis of Political Life?* New York: John Wiley and Sons, pp. 17-18. (ii) Gabriel A. Almond (1970). "A Functional Approach to Comparative Politics", in Gabriel A. Almond and James S. Coleman (eds): *The Politics of Developing Areas*. Princeton: Princeton University Press, Paperback Edn., p. 7, originally published by Princeton University Press in 1960. *Comparative Politics—A Developmental Approach*. New Delhi: Amerind Publishing Co., Indian Reprint, 1975, pp. 19-21, Originally published by Little Brown & Co, Boston (USA) in 1966.
3. David Easton. (i) "An Approach to the Analysis of Political Systems", *World Politics*, Vol. IX. No. 3, (April 1957), pp. 383-399. (ii) *A Framework for Political Analysis*. Englewood Cliffs, N.J.: Prentice Hall, Inc, 1965. (iii) *A Systems Analysis of Political Life*. New York: John Wiley & Sons, 1965.
4. Gabriel A. Almond. (i) "A Functional Approach to Comparative Politics", in Gabriel A. Almond & James S. Coleman (eds) *The Politics of Developing Areas*, Princeton, N.J., Princeton University Press, 1960. (ii) *Comparative Politics—A Developmental Approach*. Boston: Little Brown & Co, 1966 in collabouration with G.B. Powell Jr.
5. David Easton. *A Framework for Political Analysis, Op. cit.*, p. 57.
6. *Ibid.*, p. 96.
7. David Easton. *A System Analysis of Political Life, Op. cit*, p. 23.

8. *Ibid.*, p. 32.
9. *Ibid.*, p. 21.
10. *Ibid.*, p. 38.
11. *Ibid.*, p. 159.
12. *Ibid.*, pp. 159-60.
13. *Ibid.*, p. 165.
14. *Ibid.*, p. 177.
15. *Ibid.*, p. 179.
16. *Ibid.*, p. 212.
17. *Ibid.*, p. 29.
18. *Ibid.*, p. 30.
19. *Ibid.*, p. 33.
20. *Ibid.*, p. 57.
21. *Ibid.*, pp. 156-57, 220.
22. *Ibid.*, p. 59.
23. *Ibid.*
24. *Ibid.*, p. 220.
25. David Easton. *A Framework for Political Analysis, Op. cit.*, p. 93.
26. David Easton. *A Systems Analysis of Political Life, Op. cit.*, pp. 85-149.
27. *Ibid.*, pp. 272-273.
28. *Ibid.*, p. 273.
29. *Ibid.*
30. *Ibid.*, p. 301.
31. *Ibid.*, pp. 247-49, 343-47.
32. Gabriel A. Almond (1960). "Introduction: A Functional Approach to Comparative Politics" in Gabriel A. Almond and James S. Coleman (eds), *The Politics of Developing Areas* (Princeton, N.J.: Princeton University Press. Paperback edn, 1970, p. 7.
33. Gabriel A. Almond and G.B. Powell Jr. (1966). *A Developmental Approach*. Boston: Little Brown & Co. Indian Reprint, New Delhi: Amerind Publishing Co., 1975, pp. 20-21.
34. *Ibid.*, p. 25.
35. *Ibid.*, p. 26.
36. *Ibid.*, p. 27.
37. *Ibid.*, p. 29.
38. *Ibid.*
39. *Ibid.*
40. *Ibid.*, p. 30.
41. Gabriel A. Almond. "Introduction: A Functional Approach to Comparative Politics" in Gabriel A. Almond and James S. Coleman (eds.), *The Politics of Developing Areas, Op. cit.*, p. 12.

42. *Ibid.*, p. 11.
43. *Ibid.*
44. *Ibid.*, p. 11 and p. 18.
45. Gabriel A. Almond. *Comparative Politics: A Developmental Approach, Op. cit.*, p. 28.
46. *Ibid.*, p. 29.
47. *Ibid.*, p. 201.
48. *Ibid.*, p. 38 and p. 207.
49. Gabriel A. Almond and Sindey Verba (1963). *The Civic Culture.* Princeton, N.J.: Princeton University Press. 4th Printing, 1972, p. 14.
50. *Ibid.*, p. 33.

6

Political Culture Theory

Politics of a Society may be analyzed in cultural perspective. This academic endeavour undertaken on employing the cultural approach seems to have facilitated the formulation of the Political Culture Theory of Politics. In this context, there may be noted the contribution of some eminent scholars such as Gabriel A. Almond, Sidney Verba, James S. Coleman, Lucian W. Pye, Fred I. Grennstein, Dennis Kavanagh, G.B. Powell Jr, and others. Among them, the pioneering theorist seems to be Gabriel A. Almond.

The Concept of Political Culture

Political Culture is a distinct dimension of the overall pattern of Culture of a Society. Societal Culture, as Edward B. Taylor[1] elucidates, is that simplex whole which includes knowledge, belief, art, morals, law, custom and any other capabilities and habits acquired by man as a member of a society." It is also conceptualized by Raymond W. Firth[2] as a distinct pattern of orientations born out of a shared way of life of an organized set of individuals, and it tends to shape their interactions and social relationships. Similarly, E. K. Wilson[3] points out that it consists of all such knowledge, values, and beliefs, both existential and normative, which are socially shared and transmitted from generation to generation. Thus, on the whole, culture represents shared psychological orientations of the people of a Society towards societal objects; and it seems to be a vital determinant of the total societal life as well as the dynamics of all institutions and systems of the Society including the Social System, the Economic System, and the Political System. Therefore, the Societal Culture is the web that binds together the people of a Society; and simultaneously it tends to shape and determine the societal dynamics.[4]

In the overall pattern of Culture of a Society, there may be discerned and noted a distinct type relating to Politics, what may be termed as its 'Political Culture'. It is defined by Gabriel A. Almond, the founding father of this nomenclature, as "a particular pattern of orientations to political action."[5] On elabourating it, he explains: "...Political Culture... is a set of attitudes-cognitions, value-standards, and feelings—towards the political system, its various roles and role-incumbents. It also includes knowledge of, values affecting, and feelings towards the inputs of demands and claims into the Political System, and its authoritative outputs."[6] More precisely, he points out: "When we speak of political culture of a society we refer to the political system as internalized in the cognitions, feelings, and evaluations of its population."[7] According to Almond, Politics of a Society emerges when its Political System becomes dynamic owing to the formation and transmission of people's demands on various societal issues, conversion of these demands by the Authorities into authoritative decisions, and implementation of these decisional outputs effectively on the people. However, the overall dynamics of the Political System tends to be crucially influenced and determined by the people's political behaviour and roles which are, indeed, shaped by the patterns of their political orientations or Political Culture. Hence, the pattern of the Political Culture of the people, by way of shaping their political behaviour and roles, tends to influence significantly the dynamics of the Political system in respect of its stability, change, or entropy. The congruent pattern of Political Culture would produce supportive political behaviour towards the Political System, and would, most likely, contribute towards its stability and viability; whereas the alienated pattern of Political Culture would produce unfavourable and inimical behaviour towards the Political System, and would, most likely, help-create a situation of political instability and change. Therefore, Almond[8] considers 'the Pattern of Political Culture' as the vital determinant of both Micro-politics (political behaviour of the individual), and Macro-politics (Dynamics of the Political System).

Similarly, Political Culture is defined by Sidney Verba as "all politically relevant orientations.... orientations to all aspects of politics."[9] He elabourates: "The Political culture of a society consists of the system of empirical beliefs, expressive symbols, and values which defines the situation in which political action takes place."[10] He further explains: "As we use the term political culture, it refers to the system of beliefs about patterns of political interactions and institutions. It refers not to what is happening in the world of politics, but what people believe about these happenings. And these beliefs can be of several kinds; they can be empirical beliefs about what actual state of political life is; they can be beliefs as to the goals or values that ought to be pursued in political life; and these beliefs may have an important expressive or emotional dimension. Political Culture forms an important link between the events of politics and the behaviour of individuals in relation to these events."[11] Thus, according to Verba, the pattern of Political Culture serves as a determining system of control[12] for individual's political behaviour and also for the working of the Political System.

Political Culture is also defined by Lucian W. Pye as the coherent pattern of individuals' "attitudes, sentiments, and cognition that inform and govern political behaviour in any society."[13] On the determining impact of Political Culture on Politics, he explains: "For the individual the political culture provides controlling guidelines for effective political behaviour and for the collectivity it gives a systematic structure of values and rational considerations which ensures coherence in the performance of institutions and organizations."[14] Pye[15], thus, emphasizes that Political Culture which constitutes the psychological and subjective realm of Politics gives meaning to the Polity, form to the Political Process, discipline to Political Institutions, and relevance to Individual's Political Roles.

Likewise, Fred I. Greenstein[16] conceptualizes Political Culture as patterns of political orientations comprising the individuals' dispositions, beliefs, and attitudes towards political objects such as citizen-role, subject-role, and specialized-role in the Political System. This conceptualization is also upheld by Dennis Kavanagh[17] when he defines Political Culture as "the emotional and attitudinal environment within which the political system operates."

Thus, despite differences among the scholars as to the political objects that constitute the central themes of Political Culture, there may be noted a general consensus that the nomenclature 'Political Culture' connotes the individuals' patterns of political psychology or mind-set which tend to condition and shape their political behaviour and roles, and simultaneously, the pattern and styles of performance of the Political System.

Political Culture: A Scheme for Empirical Characterization

For the purpose of characterization of Political Culture in empirical or real-world situation in a Society, the proposition of Gabriel A. Almond and Sidney Verba seems to provide the most convenient guidelines. It is presented in their pioneering work entitled 'The Civic Culture'[18] in which they propose that the pattern of Political Culture may be empirically characterized and discerned on enquiring into the individual's political orientations specifically in relation to the political objects and the political process of his Society. According to Almond and Verba, there are three major components[19] of an orientation, and these are (i) Cognition, (ii) Affect, and (iii) Evaluation. Cognition refers to the level of knowledge and awareness, accurate or otherwise, towards an object. Affect refers to the feeling of attachment to or alienation from the object, and Evaluation refers to the opinion or judgment on the concerned object as to whether it is good or bad, right or wrong, and just or unjust. These three dimensions of an orientation need to be empirically enquired into in respect of major types of political objects. As regards the political objects, Almond and Verba identify four major types[20] such as (i) the National Political System as a General Object, (ii) the Input Objects, (iii) the Output Objects, and (iv) the Self as an Actor in the Political Process of the concerned Society. The following Figure presents the way of empirical characterization of Political Culture.[21]

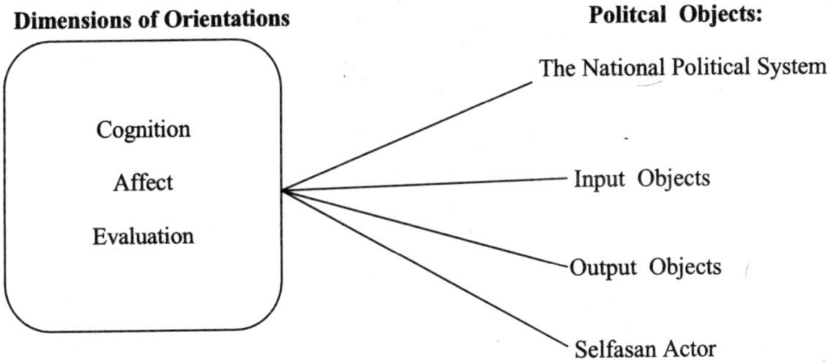

Thus, the individual's patterns of orientation including his Cognition, Affect, and Evaluation are to be enquired into and ascertained in respect of each of the four broad types of Political Objects such as the National Political System in general, the Input Objects, the Output Objects, and the Self as an Actor in the Political Process of his Society. For instance, the pattern of cognition of the individual, whether accurate or otherwise, towards the National Political System, in general, with its distinct features such as its constitutional characteristics, history, size, location etc. may be enquired into. Simultaneously, there may be enquired into and ascertained the individual's pattern of Affect or feeling of attachment or alienation, and also the pattern of his Evaluation or judgment on his National Political System in general. Likewise, there may be enquired into and ascertained, the individual's patterns of Cognition, Affect, and Evaluation towards the Input Objects such as the Pressure Groups and Political Parties and their roles in the process of interest-articulation and interest-aggregation respectively, and also towards the Output Objects such as the Legislature, the Executive, and the Judiciary, and their roles, respectively, in the process of performance of the functions of rule-making, rule-application, and rule-adjudication respectively. Moreover, the attitudinal pattern including Cognition, Affect and Evaluation of the individual towards his own Self as an Actor in respect of his Rights. Duties, and Roles in the Political Process, and also his 'Subjective Sense of Political Competence and Efficacy' may be enquired into and ascertained.

Such an exploration of the individual's patterns of orientation including Cognition, Affect, and Evaluation towards the National Political System in general, the Input Objects, the Output Objects, and the Political Self as an Object may enable the researcher to characterize empirically, and that too, conveniently the Patterns of Political Culture of the Individual as well as the Collectivity or people of a Society.

A Typology of Political Culture: Almond's Model

Political Culture, in the real-word situations, may be classified into different types and kinds. In this context, scholarly endeavours are found to be many and varied. However, the Typology of Political Culture as conceptualized by Gabriel A. Almond seems to be the most convenient and relevant one for the purpose of undertaking empirical research works, and political analysis.

The theoretical basis of Almond's Typology of Political Culture is manifest in his proposition: "The political culture of a nation is the particular distribution of patterns of orientation towards political objects among the members of the nation."[22] According to Almond, the type of Political Culture may be discerned on ascertaining the pattern of distribution of orientations of the individual towards the political objects. Therefore, this intellectual endeavour involves an enquiry into the patterns of cognitive, affective, and evaluative orientation of the individual towards the four broad types of political objects such as the National Political System in general, the Input Objects, the Output Objects, and the Self as an Actor in the political process of the Society. Such an exploration would reveal the pattern of distribution of political orientations in the individual's mind or psychology. On this basis, Almond theoretically discerns the Pure-types of Political Culture.

Pure-Types of Political Culture

The following table presents a theoretical typology of the ideal or Pure-Types of Political Culture on the basis of the particular distribution of patterns of political orientations in the individual's mind.

Pure-Types of Political Culture[23]

Types of Political Culture	**Orientations towards the Political Objects**			
	The National Political System	**Input Objects**	**Output-Objects**	**The Self as an Object**
Parochial Political Culture	0	0	0	0
Subject Political Culture	I	0	1	0
Participant Political Culture	1	1	1	1

Basing on the particular distribution of orientations towards the types of Political Objects, Almond theoretically classifies Political Culture into three ideal or Pure Types[24] such as (i) Parochial Political Culture, (ii) Subject Political Culture, and (iii) Participant Political Culture. When the individual's pattern of orientations towards the above four types of political objects reveal utter ignorance or lack of awareness, the pattern of his Political Culture may be typified as the Parochial Political Culture. Such an individual does not have cognition of his National Political System, its Input and Output Objects, and also, of his own Self as an Actor with Rights, Duties, and Roles in the Political Process of his Society. Lacking in cognition of the political objects, he does not have affect and evaluation towards these objects. A Parochial Individual is, thus, completely ignorant of this National Political Process of his Society, but he is exclusively concerned with his family and local affairs. As different from the Parochial Political Culture, the Subject Political Culture is characterized by a pattern of distribution of orientations in which the individual is exclusively oriented towards his National Political System and the Output Objects, but he does not have cognition of the Input Objects and his own Self as an Actor in the Political Process. Such an individual is aware of his National Political System and its Output Objects only, and he forms positive affect and evaluation towards these objects, but lacking in cognition of the Input Objects and himself as a Political Actor, he does not participate in the political process of his Society. Thus, he forms essentially a passive relationship with his Political System, and simply renders obedience to it. As different from this pattern of Subject Political Culture, there may be discerned another pattern of distribution of political orientations, what may be termed as 'the Participant Political Culture', if the individual is oriented towards all the four types of political objects, and forms affect and evaluation, whether positive or negative, towards the National Political System, its Input and Output objects, and himself as a Political Actor. Such an individual is actively oriented towards himself as a Political Actor because he cognizes of his Rights, Duties and Roles in the Political Process, and he also possesses a high sense of Political Efficacy and Competence. Hence, he participates, actively in the Political Process of his Society.

Thus, Almond formulates a scheme of classification of the Ideal or Pure-Types of Political Culture. He also postulates that each type is not an exclusive type in the sense that it does not replace other types as, for instance, the Participant Political Culture does not replace or exclude the Subject Political Culture and the Parochial Political Culture; and the Subject Political Culture does not replace or exclude the Parochial Political Culture. Rather, the Subject Political Culture includes the Parochial orientations and allegiance of the individual to his primary social structures such as the family, and the racial, ethnic, caste, tribal, language and religious groups etc. Similarly, the Participant Political Culture includes the individual's subject and parochial orientations. Of course, these three Pure-Types of Political Culture are arranged in an hierarchical order in which the Parochial Political Culture remains at the lowest level that may be elevated or upgraded to the level of the Subject Political Culture on acquisition of subject orientations by the Parochial individual; whereas the Participant Political Culture stands at the highest level as it includes both the subject and parochial orientations.

These Pure-Types of Political Culture, according to Almond are, however, ideal types because, in reality, no individual is found to have in him any one type of orientation to the exclusion of the other types; rather the Parochial, the Subject, and the Participant Orientations are found to be present in every individual, of course, in different proportions and amount. Hence, on the basis of the predominant orientation in his psychology, he may be culturally characterized as a Parochial, or a Subject, or a Participant Individual. For instance, an individual may be typified as a Parochial-Individual provided he is predominantly parochial in orientation, whereas he may be typified as a Subject-Individual if he possesses subject orientations predominantly, and he may be typified as a Participant-Individual if the participant-orientations are present in him predominantly. Thus, Almond notices the phenomenon of "Cultural-mix"[25] at the level of the individual. He also observes it at the level of the collectivity or the mass of people of a Society, and finds that its total population may consist of the Participant, the Subject and the Parochial Individuals in different numerical sizes. On the basis of the numerical configuration of these three cultural types of individuals of a Society, the overall mixed-type of its Political Culture, according to Almond, may be empirically discerned and typified.

Mixed-Types of Societal Political Culture

Basing on the phenomenon of 'Cultural-Mix ' that characterizes the people of a Society, Almond classifies 'Societal Political Culture', in the real-world situation, into four 'Systemically Mixed Types'[26] such as: (i) the Parochial-Subject Political Culture, (ii) the Subject-Participant Political Culture, (iii) the Parochial-Participant Political Culture, (iv) the Civic Culture.

The Parochial-Subject Political Culture characterizes the Pattern of Political Culture of a Society where most of its people possess parochial orientations predominantly, yet a small segment of its population is found to have formed subject-orientations in them in the sense that they are additionally oriented to the centralized Authority of their Polity and its Output Objects such as the Executive, the Legislature, and the Judicial Institutions. For example, such a Type of Political Culture characterized the people of the erstwhile Ottoman Empire of the Medieval Age. As different from this type, the Subject-Participant Political Culture characterizes a Society where most of its people possess subject-orientations predominantly, yet a small segment of its population is found to have formed participant orientations in them in the sense that they intend to participate actively in the political process of their Society. However, this emerging stratum of the population with participant orientations remains as the democratic-aspirants only either because of lack of participant structures such as parties, and a free electoral system or because of frequent suspension of these structures by the Authoritarian Rulers. This Type of Political Culture characterized many Societies during the Nineteenth Century as, for instance, France, Italy and Germany. Distinguished from this type, there may be noted the Parochial-Participant Political Culture that characterizes a Society where most of its people have formed participant orientations, and they participate actively in the political process through the participant-input structures such as parties, pressure groups, and the electoral system, yet they retain very strong parochial allegiances to the primordial institutions such as the racial, ethnic, caste, tribal familial, linguistic and religious groups etc. that tend to influence significantly their participant-roles in the national political process. These people tend to uphold and promote their parochial allegiances and interest even at the cost the national interests. Consequently, the participant or democratic structures become unable to function democratically, in the true sense of the term, as these are over-influenced by parochial allegiances and interests. This Type of Political Culture is found to characterize most of the 'New Nations' that have emerged in Asia, Africa, Latin-America, and the Middle East in the Post-World War-II period.

Distinguished from the above three Mixed-Types of Political Culture, there may be noted 'The Civic Culture'[27] which is characterized by a harmonious blending and synthesis of the parochial, the subject, and the participant orientations in the individual. It is a distinct pattern of political orientation that induces the individual to participate actively and allegiantly in the National Political Process while simultaneously retaining his subject orientations and also, his parochial allegiances. As such, 'The Civic Individual' on being allegiantly-oriented to his National Political System makes demands on various societal issues, becomes a member of pressure-groups and political parties, and participates actively and regularly in the electoral process in electing his representatives to form the Government. Of course, while playing his participatory roles, he renders obedience to the decisions of his Political System, and retains his parochial allegiances, yet he always upholds and promotes the national interests, if necessary, on compromising and sacrificing his parochial interests. Thus, his participant-orientations harmoniously combine with, but do not replace, his subject and parochial orientations, and his Political Culture becomes essentially characterized by national and rational political-orientations. As such, the Civic Culture is 'an allegiant participant culture'[28] that orients the individual positively to his Political System, its Input and Output Structures, and his own Political-Self actively. It, thus, represents a balanced and harmonious synthesis of political activity, rationality, and national allegiance, with allegiance to parochial institutions and values. This type of Political Culture, in the real-world situations, is noticed in some contemporary developed societies such as the U.K. and the U.S.A.

Thus, Almonds' Typology, of 'Systemically-mixed Political Culture' provides useful guidelines for discerning and typifying empirically the Patterns of Political Culture of different Societies of this World.

Political Culture and Political Socialization

Patterns of Political Culture are formed in the individuals or people of a Society through the process of 'Political Socialization'. It may be defined as the process of political learning through which patterns of Political Culture or Political Orientations are learned and acquired by the individuals. Hence, Political Culture and Political Socialization are interlinked, and therefore, it becomes imperative to comprehend the 'Political Socialization Process' and to enquire into its implications in the context of formation of patterns of Political Culture in the people.

Political Socialization is defined by David Easton[29] as those developmental processes through which individuals acquire political orientations and patterns of behaviour. It is also defined by Gabriel A. Almond[30] as 'the process of induction into the political culture.' It is also elucidated by Fred I. Greenstein[31] as that process which "encompasses all political learning, formal and informal, deliberate and unplanned, at every stage of the life cycle, including not only explicitly political learning but also nominally non-political learning of politically relevant personality characteristics". Since learning is essentially 'an interaction-acquisition process'[32], Political Socialization involves the learning of both explicitly political orientations and politically relevant non-political orientations by the individual as and when he interacts with various political socializers or agents; and consequently, there is formed in him patterns of Political Culture. As such, Political Socialization may be undertaken by the Political Socializers through two different forms[33] such as (i) the Manifest Form, and (ii) the Latent Form.

When the Political Socializers undertake political socialization of the individual on transmitting explicitly political orientations and values, the form of political learning may be termed as the Manifest Form; whereas the Latent Form involves the Socializers' transmission of non-political orientations and values that help form politically relevant attitudinal patterns and personality-traits in the individual. Thus, in the entire process of Political Socialization, significant roles are played by the Political Socializers or Agents in the context of formation of patterns of Political Culture in the individuals and collectivities. Moreover, it needs to be noted that Political Socialization is a life-long process of political learning, and that various Political Socializers tend to play their roles in different forms, and with varying impact at different stages of the individual's life in forming and shaping patterns of Political Culture in him However, in the individual's life, there may be noted the significant roles of some universal socializers or agents such as Family, School, Peer-Group, Mass-media, Secondary Groups, and the Political Milieu or Environment.

Role of Political Socializers

The Political Socializers undertake political socialization of the individual through both the Manifest Form and the Latent Form. However, they tend to accord greater importance to one form, as against the other, in consideration of the individual's cognitive maturity that usually proceeds with his biological maturity. In the context of the individual's biological maturity, there may be discerned two major phases[34] in his life, and these are (i) the Pre-adult phase, and (ii) the Adult Phase. During the pre-adult phase which includes the childhood and the adolescence of the individual, the socializers tend to accord greater importance to the Latent Form than the Manifest Form because of the cognitive immaturity of the socializee to comprehend explicitly political values and messages. In this context of the political socialization of the pre-adult, there may be noted the significant roles of two great and universal socializers such as the Family and the School which tend to play their roles mostly through the latent form in transmitting to the socializee non-political orientations and values with subsequent political consequences and implications for him.

The Family is the first Socializer to transmit, and to help-form initial orientations and belief-system in the child. Its impact tends to be immense and everlasting because the Parents are the first persons with whom the child interacts, and also because of his complete dependence on the parents for satisfaction of basic needs of life such as food, clothes, shelter, affection, and bodily-protection. Hence, the child, on viewing his parents as significant persons[35], tends to obey and imitate them, and to perform gratification-eliciting activities. Moreover, the child's emotional attachment with his parents, and his regular interactions with them create the most congenial environment for him to learn parental values, orientations, and their belief-system. Hence, the child comes to learn his family's social identities in respect of race, ethnicity, caste, tribe, language, religion and class etc. These social identities may serve as very important referral variables[36] for his subsequent political behaviour and roles during adulthood. Moreover the 'Parental Authority Structure'[37], whether democratic or authoritarian, may influence significantly the formation of the child's personality that would be politically relevant during adulthood. The Parental Authority-Structure may be termed as the authoritarian pattern if the Parents demand unquestioning obedience from the child, and impose their decisions and orders rigidly on him; whereas it may be termed as the democratic pattern if the Parents treat the child with affection, and allow and encourage him to participate actively in the family's affairs and issues. Since, the Parents constitute the family's 'Authority Structure', the child is most likely to learn authority-orientations corresponding to his Parental Authority-Structure, and may form his personality-traits, whether democratic or authoritarian, accordingly. Thus, the Family may undertake latent political socialization of the child on transmitting effectively some crucial non-political values and orientations that may subsequently be politically relevant for him during adulthood. Simultaneously, the Family, to some extent, may undertake manifest political socialization of the child provided he participates in, or listens to parental discussions on explicitly political values, ideologies, or political affairs concerning the Society.

During the pre-adult-phase, there may also be noted the significant role of another socializer—the 'School' which undertakes both latent and manifest political socialization of the child and the adolescent through some important agencies[38] and mechanisms such as the Curriculum, the Teacher, the School-rituals, the School Social-Milieu, and the School Extra curricular activities. The School provides formal education and instructions to its students by the Teacher who teaches them on the basis of a structured curriculum or syllabus. Since the basic requirement of the classroom teaching is maintenance of discipline and order, the students tend to learn and practice these non-political values in the School. Moreover, through their regular interactions with the Teacher in the classroom, they tend to learn authority-orientations, whether authoritarian or democratic, corresponding to the Teacher's Authority-Pattern. Simultaneously, through their interactions with the fellow class-mates, they tend to learn the non-political value of cooperation or conflict and discrimination which is transmitted by the social-milieu or social composition of the student-population. For instance, heterogeneous composition of the student-population in terms of social variables of race, ethnicity, tribe, caste, gender, language, religion, class etc. may influence the students to learn the non-political value of cooperation and tolerance; whereas homogenous composition of the student-population in respect of their social identity may influence them to learn the value of discrimination, intolerance, and conflict. Similarly, the students, through their participation in the extra-curricular activities, may learn the non-political values of active participation and cooperation. Learning of all these non-political values and orientations may be politically relevant for them when they would play political roles during adulthood. Thus, the School undertakes mostly the latent political socialization of the students. However, it may also undertake, to some extent, their manifest political socialization through the curriculum which may contain courses on civics, citizenship, government, and political ideology. Moreover, observation of public-rituals such as celebration of the Independence Day, the Republic Day, the Human Rights Day, and the Birthdays of National Leaders etc. may serve to transmit explicitly political values to the students during their pre-adult phase of life, and contribute to the process of their manifest political socialization.

During the adult phase of the individual, some important Socializers such as the Mass-media, the Peer Group, the Secondary Groups, and the Political-Milieu tend to undertake mostly his manifest political socialization because of his cognitive maturity that usually increases with biological maturity and makes him capable of understanding explicitly political values and messages. In this context, it may be noted that the Mass-media such as News-Papers, Television, Radio, Books, and Magazines etc. transmit explicitly political news, views, and information to the people quickly and easily, and tend to form patterns of political orientations in them. Similarly, the Peer Groups which are composed of close and intimate friends, and also the Secondary Groups which include both occupational interest groups and political parties tend to undertake manifest political socialization of their members through discussions on explicitly political values, ideologies, and public policies. Moreover, the Political-Milieu of the Society tends to create awareness and opinions on its political issues and affairs in the people who get exposed to it, and consequently, patterns of political orientations are formed in them.

Thus, various Political Socializers tend to socialize the people, both manifestly and latently, in varieties of political values and orientations at different stages of their life[39], and consequently, Patterns of Political Culture are formed in them. These Patterns of Political Culture tend to shape and condition significantly their political behaviour and roles which, in turn, influence to a very great extent, the dynamics of the Political System.

Political Culture and the Political System

The overall Pattern of Political Culture of a Society and its Political System seem to be greatly interlinked in the sense of their reciprocal influences and interpretation. The interlinkage emerges because of the fact that the Political System is embedded on a distinct Pattern of Political Culture[40] which is congruent to its Structure or Form. Hence, it becomes imperative to discern the Patterns of 'Culture-Structure Relationship'. In this context, according to Almond[41], there may be discerned three types of relationship such as (i) Relationship of Allegiance or Congruence, (ii) Relationship of Apathy, and (iii) Relationship of Alienation. Each of these Patterns of Culture-Structure Relationship is characterized by distinct patterns of orientations in respect of 'Cognition, Affect, and Evaluation' of the people towards the Political System as a whole, including its General Features, Input Objects, Output Objects, and the Individual's Political-Self as an Object. These are presented symbolically in the following table:

Types of Culture-Structure Relationship[42]

Overall Patterns of Political Orientations	Type of Relationships		
	Allegiance	Apathy	Alienation
Cognitive Orientation	+ (Accurate)	+ (Accurate)	+ (Accurate)
Affective Orientation	+ (Positive)	0 (Indifference)	- (Negative)
Evaluational Orientation	+ (Positive)	0 (Indifference)	- (Negative)

The Pattern of Culture-Structure Relationship may be typified as Allegiant (Congruent) Relationship provided the political cognitive orientations of the people, in general, are accurate, and their affective and evaluational orientations are positive (supportive) towards the Political System. On the contrary, if the people cognize the political objects, but their affective and evaluational orientations approach zero or indifference, the Pattern of Culture-Structure Relationship may be typified as the Relationship of Apathy; and if the people are cognitively oriented towards the political objects, but their affective and evaluational orientations become negative (unsupportive), the Pattern of Culture-Structure Relationship may be typified as the Relationship of Alienation. These different Patterns of Culture-Structure Relationship seem to be immensely crucial in influencing the dynamics of the Political System in the context of its stability and viability or transformation and change. In case of the Allegiant (congruent) Pattern of Culture-Structure Relationship, the Political System would, most likely, remain stable and viable because it has supported the Political Culture and the consequent supportive political behaviour of its people. On the contrary, the Apathetic Pattern of Culture-Structure Relationship where people become indifferent to the Political System, there is initiated the process of political instability; and when there emerges the Alienated Pattern of Culture-Structure Relationship, people become highly dissatisfied and unsupportive to the Political System, and consequently, there would, most likely, occur political instability entailing change and transformation of the Political System as desired and demanded by the people.

Thus, the Pattern of Societal Political Culture and its 'Relationship with the Structure' or Form of the Political System tend to influence significantly the political dynamics of a Society. Simultaneously, the Political System also tends to generate and foster the Allegiant (Congruent) Pattern of Political Culture in the people as it is necessary for its very survival, stability, and viability. This endeavour is undertaken by the Political System through the Process of Political Socialization in inducting the 'Congruent Pattern of Political Culture'[43] in the people. Therefore, an empirical analysis of Politics, in cultural perspective, necessarily involves an enquiry into the Pattern of Political Culture of the people as acquired by them through the process of political socialization. It also involves, simultaneously, a scrutiny of the impact of the Pattern of People's Political Culture on the dynamics of the Political System.

A Critical Evaluation

For characterizing Political-Culture Empirically, Almond identifies four broad categories of Political Objects such as the Political System as a General object, the Input Objects, the Output Objects, and the Self as an Object in the political process; and he proposes an orientational enquiry of these Objects in respect of Cognition, Affect, and Evaluation of the Individual. However, even though this formulation seems to be scientifically designed and academically most relevant, the outcome of the enquiry may become vague and untrue in characterizing the pattern of Political Culture of the Individual and the Collectivity because the responses of the Respondents may be superficial, non-serious, non-relevant, and casual. Since human psychology is complex and complicated, the Respondents may not ventilate true, relevant, and adequate information in responding to the questions and queries of the researcher. Hence, because of lack of true and relevant information, the findings and the conclusion may be untrue, and misleading in characterizing the pattern of Political Culture in real-world situations.

Moreover, Almond, on characterizing 'the Civic Culture' as the 'Allegiantly-Participant Culture', presents it as the Developed and Modern Political Culture of a Society. But he does not explain as to why 'Allegiantly-Participant Orientation' constitutes the hallmark of the Modern Political Culture. If the Political Culture of an Individual or Collectivity would be devoid of allegiant orientation towards the Political System, would it be characterized as non-modern political culture? Such a characterization would certainly classify the pattern of political culture of the people of most of the Societies of the World in the category of non-modern political culture. Therefore, the attribute of allegiance should not be associated with the pattern of modern political culture.

However, despite these lacunae and shortcomings, the Theory of Political Culture of Gabriel A. Almond is a pioneering academic endeavour in the context of analyzing Politics scientifically, and that too, in cultural perspective.

Notes

1. Edward B. Taylor (1968). "Quoted by Milton Singer in 'Culture'" in David L. Sills (ed.), *International Encyclopaedia of Social Sciences*. New York: The Macmillan & the Free Press, Vol. III, p. 527.
2. Raymond W. Firth (1961). *Elements of Social Organization*. London: Watts, p. 27.
3. E. K. Wilson (1966). *Sociology—Rules, Roles and Relationships*. Illinois: Dorsey Press, p. 51.
4. Marvin E. Olsen (1968). The Process of Social Organization. New York: Halt, Rinehart & Winston, Indian Reprint. New Delhi: Oxford & IBH Publishing Co, 1975, p. 62.
5. Gabriel A. Almond (1956). "Comparative Political System", *The Journal of Politics*, Vol. 18, No. 3, p. 396.
6. Gabriel A. Almond (1960). "A Functional Approach to Comparative Politics", in Gabriel A. Almond & James S. Coleman (eds.), *The Politics of Developing Areas*. Princeton, N.J.: Princeton University Press. Paperback Edition by the same Publishers, 1970, pp. 27-28.
7. Gabriel A. Almond (1963). The Civic Culture (Princeton, N.J.: Princeton, University Press, 4th Printing, By the same Publishers, 1972, p. 14.
8. Gabriel A. Almond. *Ibid.*, pp. 32-33.
9. Sidney Verba (1965). "Comparative Political Culture" in Lucian W. Pye & Sidney Verba (eds.), *Political Culture and Political Development*. Princeton, N.J.: Princeton University Press. Paperback edition. By the same Publishers, 1969, p. 518.
10. Sidney Verba. *Ibid.*, p. 513.
11. *Ibid.*, p. 516.
12. *Ibid.*, p. 517.
13. Lucian W. Pye. "Political Culture and Political Development" in Lucian W. Pye and Sidney Verba (eds), *Political Culture and Political Development; Op. cit.*, p. 7.
14. Lucian W. Pye. *Ibid.*, p. 7.
15. *Ibid.*
16. Fred I. Greenstein (1968). "Political Socialization", in David L. Sills (ed.), *International Encyclopaedia of the Social Sciences*. New York: The Macmillan and the Free Press, Vol. 14, p. 552.
17. Dennis Kavanagh (1972). *Political Culture*. London: The Macmillan Press, p. 10.

18. Gabriel A. Almond & Sidney Verba. *The Civic Culture, Op. cit.* Specifically, p. 13.
19. Gabriel A. Almond & Sidney Verba. *Ibid.*, p. 15.
20. *Ibid.*, pp. 15-16.
21. *Ibid.*, p. 16.
22. *Ibid.*, pp. 14-15.
23. *Ibid.*, p. 17.
24. *Ibid.*, pp. 17, 23.
25. *Ibid.*, p. 25.
26. *Ibid.*, pp. 22-23.
27. *Ibid.*, p. 31.
28. *Ibid.*, p. 31.
29. David Easton and Jack Dennis (1969). *Children in the Political System: Origins of Political Legitimacy.* New York: McGrow Hill, p. 7.
30. Gabriel A. Almond. "A Functional Approach to Comparative Politics" in Gabriel A. Almond and James S. Coleman (eds.), *The Politics of Developing Areas, Op. cit.*, p. 27.
31. Fred I. Greenstein (1965). "Political Socialization" in David L. Sills (ed.), *International Encyclopaedia of the Social Sciences.* New York: Crow Well-Collier, Vol. 14, p. 551.
32. Kenneth p. Langton (1972). *Political Socialization.* New York: Oxford University Press, 2nd Printing, p. 63.
33. Richard E. Dawson & Kenneth Prewitt (1969). Political Socialization (Boston: Little Brown & Co., pp. 63-64.
34. (i) Richard E. Dawson & Kenneth Prewitt. *Political Socialization, Op. cit.*, p. 43 (ii) Dean Jaros. *Political Socialization.* New York: Praeger, 1973) p. 57. (iii) Robert Weissberg (1974). *Political Leaming, Political Choice and Democratic Citizenship*, Englewood Cliffs, N.J. Prentice Hall, pp. 23-31.
35. (i) Fred I. Greenstein (1965). *Children and Politics.* New Haven: Yale University, pp. 115-118, (ii) James C. Davies (1965). "The Family's Role in Political Socialization", *Annals of the American Academy of Political and Social Sciences*, No. 361, p. 11.
36. Richard E. Dawson & Kenneth Prewitt. *Political Socialization, Op. cit.*, pp. 109-110.
37. Fred I. Greenstein (1969). *Personality and Politics.* Chicago: Markham Publishing Co., pp. 110-114.
38. Richard E. Dawson & Kenneth Prewitt. *Political Socialization, Op. cit.*, p. 146.

39. (i) Richard E. Dawson & Kenneth Prewitt. *Political Socialization, Ibid,* p. 43, (ii) Robert Weissberg (1974). *Political Leaming, Political Choice, and Democratic Citizenship*. Englewood Cliffs, N.J.: Prentice Hall, pp. 23-31.
40. Gabriel A. Almond (1956). "Comparative Political Systems", *Journal of Politics*, Vol. 18, No. 3, p. 396.
41. Gabriel A. Almond & Sidney Verba. *The Civic Culture, Op. cit.,* p. 22
42. *Ibid.*
43. Gabriel A. Almond. "A Functional Approach to Comparative Politics" in *The Politics of Developing Areas, Op. cit.,* p. 27.

7

Cybernetic Theory of Politics

The Concept of Cybernetics

The Cybernetic-Theory of Politics or the Theory of Political Cybernetics is the outcome of the employment of the Cybernetic Theory to the analysis of Politics of a Society. The Cybernetic Theory is originally a Theory of the Science of Mathematics. It is first conceptualized by a Mathematician named Norbert Weiner[1] who coined the word Cybernetic from the Greek word 'kubernetes' meaning 'steersman'; and basing on it, he designs the Theory of Cybernetics as a Theory of Communication and Control for the study of the dynamics of all Systems including the Physical, the Mechanical, the Biological, and the Social Systems.[2] In this context, the nomenclature 'Communication', according to him, connotes the process by which one mind or entity affects another owing to the transmission of signals, symbols, and messages.[3]

The Cybernetic Theory is, thus, designed with the Cybernetic or Communication Perspective that focuses on the transmission of infonnation, both within a System and among the Systems, as the exclusive determinant of the systemic-dynamics. This perspective or approach is borrowed by Political Scientists, and is used by them in designing the Political Cybernetic Theory for undertaking the scientific analysis of Politics of a Society. Accordingly, many intellectual endeavours have been undertaken. For instance, Karl W. Deutch views the Polity as essentially a net-work of communication of channels that functions as 'a decision and control system; and that relies upon the exchange of messages in both its domestic affairs and foreign relations for its survival and growth. Hence, he assets that the political dynamics of a Society can "only be understood through a study of messages and communications facilities which belong to it."[4] This perspective is also presented by Robert C. North[5] as he opines that State and Politics cannot exist without communications. Similarly, Gabriel A. Almond asserts : "Communication makes possible a free flow of information from the society to the polity and in the polity, from political structure to political structure. It also makes possible an open feedback from output to input again."[6] Hence, according to him, one may like the communication function to the function of circulation of blood in the body-politic[7] as it carries demands through the veins to its heart or the decision making centre, and from the heart, through the arteries, flow the outputs of rules, regulations, and adjudications that enable the polity to become dynamic, and to maintain itself. The importance of Political Communication, in the dynamics of a Political System, is also highlighted by David Easton[8] when he states that 'Political Communication' involving transmission of information from the environment to the Political System and from the Political System to the environment facilitates formation of inputs, conversion of inputs into outputs, and flow of outputs into the environment. Consequently, according to him, the Political System is enabled to work as a self-steering and self-regulating System, and to persist in a situation of either stability or change. Similarly, Lucian W. Pye[9] is of the opinion that the structure and performance of the Political System, and the level of its modernization and development tend to be crucially influenced by the communication process. Likewise, Jean Blondel, on defining political communication as "the dynamic movement of demands and decisions from one part of the political system to another"[10], asserts that "neither inputs nor outputs can take form, exist, or be related and affect the polity at large without the thread of communication."[11] According to him, "Communication links together the parts of the political system, and also the present with the past and the future so that demands are followed by policies"[12], and hence, "no operation of the Political System can take place unless the parts of the political system communicate with each other."[13] Moreover R.R. Fagen[14], R.B. Meadow[15] and Ithiel de Sola Pool[16] also highlight the tremendous importance of the communication process in influencing and conditioning the pattern of functioning of the Political System.

Thus, in the context of the communicational or cybernetic analysis of Politics, a number of Political Scientists have contributed a lot. However, there may be noted the pioneering academic endeavours of Gabriel A. Almond, and Karl. W. Deutsch who have designed meaningful and most relevant theoretical models for analyzing the political dynamics of a Society in the communicational or cybernetic perspective.

The Political Cybernetic Theory: General Features

The Political System is envisioned as an apparatus or mechanism which is capable of steering itself into action and interactions in responding to the incoming-information. It is the flow of information that enables it to work as a self-operating and also a self-regulating System while interacting with the environment. Thus, the flow of information including signals, symbols, and messages enlivens the Political System, makes it dynamic, and gives meaning and distinctiveness to the political life of its people. Therefore, the channels of communication with their nature and the content of information, indeed, constitute the basic or fundamental determinant of Politics of a Society. As such, the number and variety of channels of communication, their autonomy and fidelity in transmitting accurate and relevant information, their load capacity to transmit the volume of information, their responsiveness to the feedback information, and their combinatorial capacity to locate and associate past experience to the incoming and outgoing information do constitute the vital variables in the context of analyzing the dynamics of the Political System in the cybernetic or communicational perspective. These variables, in general, characterize the Political Cybernetic Theory. However, within it, there may be noted two different models such as: (i) the Homeostatic Model that theorizes the Political System exclusively as a Communication Apparatus, and postulates for its growth and change, and (ii) the Equilibrium Model that considers the Political Communication Function as only a vital function performed by the Political System for maintaining its Strncture and Culture in the context of its overall dynamics.

The Homeostatic Model: A Developmental Analysis

The author of the Homeostatic Model of the Cybernetic Theory of Politics is Karl W. Deutsch who, in his pioneering work "The Nerves of Government: Models of Political Communication and Control"[17], envisages the Polity or the Societal Political System as exclusively a "Cybernetic Apparatus", and explains its overall dynamics in cybernetic or communicational terms. This approach or perspective of Deutsch is founded on his fundamental assumption that Politics is the process of making decision on societal goals and of enforcing them for goal attainment.[18] Therefore, according to him, the prime concern of Politics are: (i) Decision-Making on Societal Goals, and (ii) Effective Enforcement of these Decisions. As the relevance or utility of making decisions and policies on societal goals depends on their effective enforcement, the core-area of Politics is "the area of enforceable decisions."[19] Since effective implementation of these decisions requires people's obedience and compliance, Politics, indeed, involves "the steering or manipulation of human behaviour by a combination of threats of enforcement with habits of compliance."[20] However, threats of force alone cannot constitute a durable basis of political obedience and obligation because the true basis of the Polity is 'Will' of the people, not force or coercion exercised by the Goverr.,nent on the people. Hence, voluntary obedience born out of people's 'Free Will' would facilitate effective implementation of authoritative decisions and policies, and pave for attainment of societal goals.[21] As such, the Polity and its Politics are essentially concerned with the task of forming and fostering the 'Will' for voluntary compliance and habitual obedience to the Political-Authority so that the authoritative decisions would be effectively implemented and the Political Society would be enabled to survive, grow, and develop through time. Therefore, Deutsch postulates that the essence of Politics is "the dependable co-ordination of human efforts and expectations for the attainment of the goals of the society"[22], and that the Political System is the System of "decision and control"[23] for the attainment of societal goals on securing and ensuring habitual obedience of the people to its authoritative decisions. Since the Political System, for its survival and growth, tends to depend crucially on people's habitual obedience to it, it is required to function incessantly and essentially as a mechanism of communication and social learning[24] for forming and fostering in the people their 'Will' for habitual obedience, what may be termed as legitimacy. Hence, Deutsch believes that the "inner source of political power" is legitimacy[25] which consists of "the relatively coherent and stable structure of beliefs, values, memories" for rendering habitual obedience to the Political System through the Process of Socio-Political Communication.

Thus, Deutsch, conceptualizes the Political System as essentially an evolving and developing 'Cybernetic Apparatus'[26] or a 'network of communication channels'[27] that receives and transmits information in countless ways for forming legitimacy in the people, and securing their habitual obedience. Accordingly, he designs a Model for Cybernetic Analysis of Politics, what may be termed as 'The Homeostatic Model'. It may be illustrated, in a simplified form, in the following diagram.

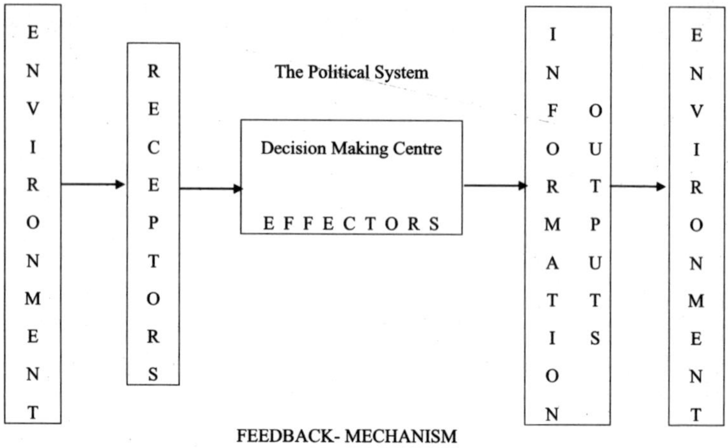

A Simplified Cybernetic (Homeostatic) Model of the Political System[28]

According to Karl W. Dutsch, the Political System, as an overall Communication Apparatus, exists and operates in a comprehensive environment and also interacts with it constantly through Communication-Structures.

Communication Structures

The Comprehensive Environment of the Political System is composed of both its National Society and the total International Society as well; and there takes place constant interactions between the Environment and the Political System through Communication Structures. In this context, the Communication Structures which play crucial roles may be classified into three major types such as: (i) the Receptors, (ii) the Effectors, and (iii)The Servo-Mechanism. These Communication Structures transmit and disseminate political and politically relevant non-political information from the Environment to the Political System, within the Political System, and also, from the Political System to the Environment.

The Receptors

The total Environment tends to influence the Political System by way of help-forming 'Information-Inputs' which consist of people's demands on varieties of societal issues including all social, economic and political issues, and their support towards the Political System. These information-inputs which originate and flow from the Environment, both domestic and foreign, are processed by some Structures such as Pressure Groups and Political Parties that may be termed as 'Receptors' of the incoming information-inputs. In processing the incoming information, the Receptors work actively in scanning, selecting, and combining these into alternative policy-proposals; and they also transmit these to the decision-making centre of the Political System for making of authoritative decisions or outputs. Consequently, the Political System is activated, and is enabled to function as a Self-Steering Apparatus.[29]

The Effectors

The Self-Operation of the Political System, thus, commences as and when its Decision-Making Centre is fed with 'Information-Inputs'; and it works as an 'Effector' for producing 'Information-Outputs 'in the form of authoritative decision and public policies. In this context, 'Effector' consists of Structures such as the Legislature, the Executive, and the Judiciary which, in reality, work as Communication-Mechanisms for processing the 'information-inputs', and producing or giving effect to the 'information-outputs' in the form of policies, laws, rules, and regulations. In this process, the Effectors scrutinize the information-inputs on the basis of relevant information available as stored up 'Memory'[30] and 'Values'[31] of the Polity. 'Memory' connotes past-information relating to governmental decisions on relevant issues made and stored up in official files, reports, and documents; whereas 'Values' connote political ideals and norms enshrined in the provisions of the Constitution of the Political System that provide guidelines for making of laws and policies for attainment of societal goals. Thus, 'Memory' and 'Values' serve as referral points for the scrutiny and selection of the 'Information-Inputs' by the 'Effectors', and for producing 'Information-Outputs'.

The Servo-Mechanism

Even though, the Political System works as a 'Self-Steering Communication Mechanism', its survival and growth through-time, seems to depend crucially upon its ability to work as a 'Self-Regulatory System'[32] by way of responding to feedback information of the people on its outputs and performance, and of changing itself, if required on the basis of such information. Self-modification seems to be greatly necessary in order to keep the people satisfied so that the Political System would acquire people's support and legitimacy, and consequently, would remain stable and viable. As such, the Political System is immensely benefitted by the 'Feedback Mechanism' which, according to Deutsch, enables it to work as a 'Servo-Mechanism'[33] or "Communication network that produces action in response to an input of information, and includes the result of its own action in the new information by which it modifies its subsequent behaviour."[34] The feedback-information[35] may be positive or negative; and it may be said to be positive if it supports and reinforces the original outputs of the Political System, whereas it may be said to be negative if it opposes the Political System's original outputs, and demands for a change in conformity with the people's will and opinion. Therefore, the Negative Feedback-Information seems to be more useful than the Positive Feedback-Information because it makes the Authorities of the Political System aware of their shortcomings and errors, and requires them to change the Outputs in conformity with the people's demands. Thus, the Political System works as a 'Servo Mechanism' or Self-Modifying Communication Mechanism that actively responds to the Negative Feedback-Information, corrects its errors, and is enabled to grow and develop through time. However, according to Deutsch, the ability of the Political System to respond successfully to the Negative Feedback-Information, and to work effectively as a Servo Mechanism tends to be crucially determined by four major factors such as Load, Lag, Gain, and Lead.[36] 'Load' refers to the volume of Negative Feedback-Information transmitted to the Government or Effector of the Political System; 'Lag' refers to the delay or time-gap that occurs between the transmission of the Negative Feedback- Information and the action taken by the Government on it; 'Gain' connotes the extent of benefit that the Political System is expected to obtain on taking corrective measures; and 'Lead' connotes the capability of the Political System as a Communication-Apparatus, to anticipate and predict accurately the consequences of non-responding to the Negative Feedback-Information. In this context, Deutsch points out, the success in goal-attainment relates inversely to the amount of Load and the extent of Lag, but positively to the amount of Gain and the extent of Lead.[37] Hence, the much the amount of Load and the wider the extent of Lag, the lesser may be the prospect of effective goal-attainment; whereas the much the amount of Gain and the higher the extent of Lead, the greater may be the prospect of attainment of goal effectively by the Political System.

Thus, the Political System functions essentially as an Open, Self-Steering, and Self-Correcting and Developing Communication-Apparatus or Cybernetic-System. However, its dynamics tends to crucially depend on extent of its Combinatorial-Richness"[38] to perform "creative intelligence function"[39] by which "information is stored, processed and evaluated."[40] According to Deutsch, the Political System receives information from three major sources: (i) from its 'Past', (ii) from its 'External Environment' including the National Society and the International Society, and (iii) from its 'Own Structures' that constitute it. These sources generate varieties of information which are transmitted through various channels; and consequently, the Political System works as an open self-steering and self-modifying entity. Hence, the Channels of Communication need not only be many and varied but also be capable of transmitting relevant information, and that too, with fidelity and accuracy. Simultaneously, the Political System is required to open up itself to receive and respond actively to the incoming-information, to evaluate its own performance on the basis of the feedback information, to develop its learning capacity and its capacity for innovation and change, and to modify its norms, form, and policies as and when necessary so as to survive, grow, and develop through time.[41]

Systemic-Homeostasis and Development

Thus, Karl. W. Deutsch designs his 'Homeostatic-Cybernetic Model' of Political System on conceptualizing the Political System as a change-prone Communication Apparatus which may change its values, norms, form and public policies, if necessary radically and frequently, in conformity with the Information-Inputs, and Feedback Information for obtaining people's legitimacy as required for its survival, viability, and development.

The Equilibrium Model: A Functional Analysis

The author of the Equilibrium Model of the Political Cybernetic Theory is Gabriel A. Almond[42] who designs it in functional perspective as deemed necessary for the maintenance of the Political System through time. According to Almond, the Political-Cybernetic or Communication Function which is performed in the context of the System's dynamics is its basic or fundamental function because its performance not only enlivens the Political System but also contributes tremendously for its maintenance and stability in respect of its overall Structure and Culture, intact, through time. On emphasizing its importance, he points out: "... it is essential in characterizing a political system to analyze the performance of the communication function. Just because of the fact that all political functions are performed by means of communication, political communication is the crucial boundary-maintenance function."[43] However, even if communication is essential for the performance of all other political functions, Almond assets: "The performance of communication function does not include all other political functions, but it constitutes instead a necessary prerequisite for the performance of other functions.[44] Its relevance may, therefore, be comprehended in respect of its utility to enliven the other Structures and Functions of the Political System, and to enable it to maintain, intact, its overall Structure (form) and Culture as necessary for attainment of stability and equilibrium.

As such, Almond's functional perspective of the 'Political Communication Phenomenon' addresses to, and delineates the various Structures which perfotm the Function of Political Communication with different styles, and also, it analyzes their implications on the attainment of the ultimate goal of Systemic-Maintenance.

Communication Structures

The Structures which perform the Function of Political Communication, according to Almond, may be classified into five major types[45] such as: (i) Informal Face-to-Face Contact, (ii) Traditional Social-Structures, (iii) Political Output-Structures, (iv) Political Input Structures, and (iv) Mass-media.

'Informal Face to Face Contact' as an Informal Channel or Structure of Communication emerge when a group of individuals gather together, and informally interact with one another. The informal interactions involve communication among them who, as a consequence, get informed of political news, views and messages both directly and indirectly. In this informal communication process, of course, the key role is played by the opinion leader who, because of his higher social status, is listened to by others with great attention and admiration. It is this opinion-leader who interprets political and public news, and transmits his views and opinions to the other members of the informal group.

'Traditional Social-Structures' are organized traditional social-groups such as, for instance, Tribal-groups, Caste-groups, Ethnic-groups, Religious-groups etc., and these groups are characterized by formal structure, enlisted membership, and selected leadership. Even though, these groups are primarily concerned with deliberations on the group-related issues, their leaders also discuss on political and public issues, and as such, they help-transmit political, and politically-relevant information to their members.

'Political Output-Structures' are formal governmental structures such as the Legislature, the Executive and the Judiciary which are primarily concerned with the enactment, administration, and adjudication of authoritative decisions or outputs of the Political System. By way of performing their primary functions, these Outputs-Structures communicate political information including messages and news to the people at large.

'Political Input-Structures' such as Pressure-Groups and Political-Parties whose primary functions are respectively interest-articulation and interest-aggregation also constitute very important Channels or Structures of Communication. Pressure-groups articulate the demands (interests) of their members, whereas Political-Parties aggregate these articulated-interests in the form of alternative policy-proposals or party-manifesto, which, indeed, constitute the basis for making of authoritative decisions by the Authority of the Political System. Thus, the Input-Structures, by way of transmitting people's demands into the Political System, tend to play vital roles in the process of Political-Communication.

Mass-media such as Newspaper, Radio, Television, Books, Magazine etc. are specialized structures which perform the Function of Political Communication as their primary function. It is through these Mass-media that the people, and also all other Structures of the Political System are specifically informed of both political information and politically relevant non-political information, and consequently, the Political System becomes dynamic.

Thus, all these five major types of Communication-Structures such as Informal Face to-Face Contact, Traditional Social-Structures, Political Output-Structures, Political Input Structures, and Mass-media are involved with transmission of political information in one way or the other, and as such, they play significant roles in the Process of Political Communication. However, the performance of the Function of Political Communication, with effectiveness and efficiency, requires autonomy[46] for them in the sense of freedom from domination and control either by the Government or by the Vested-Interest Group and Persons of the Society so that they would be enabled to transmit relevant political information with fidelity, and without distortion. Of course, among these Communication-Structures, only the Mass-media whose primary function is the function of political-communication inevitably and essentially need autonomy in order to transmit true and relevant information within the Political System, from the Environment to the Political System, and also from the Political System to the Environment. In case of control over the Mass-media by the Government or domination on them by the vested-interest groups and persons, as it happens in undemocratic and closed Political Societies, the Mass-media tend to transmit only the sponsored and selected information. Consequently, because of lack of true and relevant information, not only the efficacy and effectiveness of the Political System may decline but also, people may agitate and revolt that may create socio-political instability. Hence, the Political System, for remaining stable and viable, needs to ensure autonomy to the Communication-Structures, especially to the Mass-media, so as to enable them to transmit true and relevant information, and thereby, to create the congenial condition as necessary for maintaining and ensuring political stability and viability. For this purpose, the Political System, as Gabriel A. Almond suggests, needs to be structured democratically with democratic functions so that free-flow of information may take place. He emphatically points out: "Effective political action must be based on rational calculation which, in turn, requires information. A democratic system provides for a relatively free, multidirectional flow of information, thus making it possible for all the structures to calculate and to act effectively."[47] Moreover, the effectiveness and efficiency of the Communication-Structures, in the context of performance of the Function of Political-Communication, tend to be significantly determined by their distinct styles of communication.

Styles of Communication

The Styles of Communication which connote the various modes in which information and messages are transmitted by the

Communication Structures may be classified, according to Almond, into four major Pairs of Styles. These are: (i) Manifest or Latent Style, (ii) Specific or Diffuse Style, (iii) Particular or General Style, and (iv) Affectively-neutral or Affective Style.[48] The Manifest-Style involves transmission of an explicitly political message which is directly understood by the Audience; whereas the Latent-Style involves transmission of non-political information which may have potential political implications for the Audience. The Specific-Style involves transmission of clear political messages concerning specific political event or issue; whereas the Diffuse-Style involves transmission of information vaguely on it. The Particular-Style involves transmission of political information only to a particular individual, group or institution; whereas the General-Style involves transmission of information to all individuals and institutions of the Political Society. The Affectively-neutral Style involves transmission of objective information, free from political bias or prejudice; whereas the Affective-Style involves transmission of value-loaded political information and messages. Thus, the Communication-Structures may perform the Function of Political Communication in these various Styles or Modes. However, the Styles of Political Communication adopted by the Communication-Structures in the Modern Political Systems, according to Almond[49], are the Manifest, the Specific, the General, and the Affectively neutral Styles as against the Latent, the Diffuse, the Particular, and the Affective Styles. Moreover, along with these Modern Styles, the Communication-Structures of a Modern Polity, according to Almond[50], tend to transmit homogenous political information, and that too, with larger volume, multidirectional flow, objectivity and fidelity so that the people of the Society, and all components of the Political System would become exposed to all these relevant and true political information and messages easily and quickly. Consequently, both the Political-Inputs and Political-Outputs would be formed, and the Political System with all its components would become dynamic. Thus, the performance of the Function of Political Communication by the Communication-Strnctures, and its implications tend to be greatly significant for the dynamics of the Political System.

Implications of the Political Communication Function

The performance of the Function of Political Communication by the Communication Structures may have tremendous implications on other Functions of the Political System, and also, on the dynamics of the Political System as a whole. Other Systemic-Functions or functional aspects of the Political System, according to Almond[51], may be classified into three major categories such as: (i) Conversion-Function, (ii) System-Maintenance and Adaptation Function, (iii) Systemic-Capability.

Conversion-Functions[52] are concerned with the task of formation of Inputs and their conversion into Outputs in a Political System. These involves performance of the Input Functions of Interest-articulation and Interest-aggregation by the Pressure-Groups and the Political-Parties respectively as well as performance of the Output-Functions of Rule-making, Rule-application and Rule-adjudication respectively by the Legislature, the Executive, and the Judiciary. The performance of these six types of Conversion-Functions by their corresponding Structures requires availability of relevant and true information to each of them. For instance, the Pressure-Groups which perform the Function of Interest-articulation need to be provided with information relating to the demands and interests of their members. These articulated-demands of the people on varieties of issues need to be communicated to the Political-Parties so as to enable them to perform the Function of Interest-aggregation, and to make, accordingly, alternative policy-proposals in the form of party-manifestoes. On responding to all these political-inputs, the Legislature enacts laws, and on being informed of these legislative enactments, the Executive performs the Function of Rule-application, and the Judiciary performs the Function of Rule-adjudication. Thus, each of these sub-types of Conversion-Function may be performed by its corresponding Structure, with effectiveness and efficiency, only when each and all of them are provided with true, relevant, and adequate information. In case of non-availability or distortion of the required information, the performance of the Conversion-Functions by the corresponding Structures may be adversely affected. In such a predicament, the Political-Inputs and Outputs which are formed and processed may not enable the Political System to realize its ultimate goal of Systemic Maintenance; and lacking in people's support, the Political System is, most likely, to experience instability, entropy and disintegration.

In the context of performance of the Functions of System-Maintenance and Adaptation[53], what Almond terms as the Function of Political Socialization, the performance of the Political-Communication Function may also cast significant impact. The Function of Political-Socialization is performed by the Political-Socializers only when the Communication-Structures transmit and disseminate political and also political relevant non-political information and messages. Consequently, through the Process of Political Socialization, people learn and acquire political orientation, and dispositions, what may be termed as Patterns of Political-Culture, which help-form and condition people's political behaviour and roles, and accordingly, tend to influence the dynamics of the Political System in respect of its stability or change. In case of formation of 'Allegiant Political-Culture' in the people in the Process of Political-Communication and the allied Process of Political Socialization, the Political System would, most likely, remain stable and viable. On the contrary, formation of 'Alienated Political-Culture' in the people, through the Process of Political-Communication-cum-Political-Socialization, would, most likely, result in political instability and change because the Alienated Political-Culture would motivate people to disobey the Political System. Thus, the Communication-Structures by way of transmitting information and messages to the people tend to influence significantly the process of their political-socialization; and accordingly, there is formed in them either the pattern of allegiant political-culture or the pattern of alienated political-culture that tends to become the crucial variable for the stability or change of the Political System.

Simultaneously, the Function of Political-Communication as performed by the Communication-Structures, according to Almond, tend to determine significantly the overall dynamics of the Political System, what may be termed as 'Systemic-Capability' or 'overall performance of the political system as a distinct unit in the environment'[54] in the context of attainment of the ultimate goal of Systemic-Maintenance. Almond discerns 'Systemic Capability' into four major types[55] such as: (i) Extractive-Capability, (ii) Regulative Capability, (iii) Distributive-Capability, and (iv) Responsive-Capability. The Extractive-Capability indicates the capability of the Political System to extract goods and services from its people through taxation, levies, and also, through public recruitment of personnel as necessary for discharging its functions. The Regulative-Capability indicates its capability to regulate people's behaviour as necessary for maintenance of law, order, and peace in the Society. The Distributive-Capacity indicates its capability to distribute its resources for the good and welfare of its people. The Responsive-Capability indicates its capability to respect and obey people's will and opinions, and to be responsible to them. Among these four different types of Capabilities, however, the Responsive-Capability tends to determine significantly the three other types of Capability, and also the overall performance of the Political System as a whole. This is because the Responsive-Capability, on making the Political System responsible and responsive to the people, tends to generate in them a high sense of belongingness to, and identification with it. Consequently, people become positively and allegiantly-oriented to the Political System, and they tend to pay taxes, render services, and obey its laws, policies spontaneously. Thus, the Extractive, the Regulative and the Distributive-Capabilities are fostered and strengthened by its Responsive-Capability. However, the Responsive-Capability of the Political System seems to be greatly determined by its openness thac allows and encourages free-flow of information from the Environment into it, within it, and from the

Political System into the Environment by way of ensuring adequate autonomy to the Communication-Structures to transmit true and relevant information.

Thus, the Communication-Structures, on performing the Function of Political Communication, tend to play crucial roles in the context of the overall dynamics of the Political System which always strives to attain the ultimate goal of 'Systemic-Maintenance' in the sense of maintaining its Form and Culture intact through time. As such, the 'Equilibrium Model' of Gabriel A. Almond postulates that the Cybernetic or Communication Function is a fundamental, yet one among many other Functions of the Political System, and that it is instrumental for ensuring the Equilibrium or Maintenance of the Political System intact.

A Critical Appraisal

The Political Cybernetic-Theory, as a whole, offers both the Homeostatic-Model and the Equilibrium-Model for the purpose of undertaking the analysis of Politics of a Society specifically in the cybernetic or communication perspective. However, each one of these two models seems to be incomplete and deficient in its own when it is examined in the real-world situations. The Homeostatic-Model conceptualizes the Political system as exclusively a network of communication-channels, allows even for radical and frequent changes in the form and norms of the Political System, and thus, it completely ignores the necessity for the Political System's stability, maintenance and equilibrium. On the contrary, the Equilibrium Model is exclusively concerned with the maintenance, stability and equilibrium of the Political System, and it completely ignores the necessity and inevitability for changes in the Political System. However, in reality, it is found that every Political System incessantly strives to maintain its equilibrium and stability in respect of its Form and Norms (i.e. its structural arrangement and the congruent pattern of political-culture) because, without political stability and equilibrium, the consequence may be its collapse leading to disintegration of the

Society. Simultaneously, it is also found that no Political System can prevent political changes, and that every Political System is required to change its Norms and Form, from time to time, owing to vital changes in the socio-economic and political conditions in the Society, and the emergence of new political ideology. Thus, the need for political equilibrium is as important as the need for bringing about the required political changes. Therefore, every Political System must undertake endeavours not only to maintain its equilibrium in respect of its Form (structural arrangement) and the Congruent Political Culture but also to bring about required political changes as demanded by the people. Such an endeavour that addresses effectively to these twin needs may enable the Political System to survive and develop through time. In this endeavour, the Communication or Cybernetic Structures, on performing the Function of Political Communication, may contribute towards the capability of the Political System to synchronize its need for maintenance (equilibrium) with the need for change and development (homeostasis). Therefore, the Political-Cybernetic or communication phenomenon needs to be viewed in an integrated perspective as contributing to both the equilibrium and the homeostasis of the Political System. As such, the Equilibrium Model and the Homeostatic Model need to be suitably combined together, and the emerging 'Comprehensive Political-Cybernetic Theory' may be used for analyzing the Politics of a Society meaningfully and empirically.

Notes

1. Robert C. North (1967). "The Analytical Prospects of Communications Theory" in James C. Charlesworth (ed), *Contemporary Political Analysis*. New York: The Free Press, p. 300.
2. Norbert Weiner (1956). *The Human Use of Human beings,* Garden City: Double Day, p. 15.
3. Norbert Weiner. *Ibid.*, p. 15.
4. Karl W. Deutsch (1963). *The Nerves of Government*. New York: The Frees Press, p. 76.

5. Robert C. North. "The Analytical Prospects of Communications Theory" in James C. Charlesworth (ed.), *Contemporary Political Analysis. Op. cit.,* p. 301.
6. Gabriel A. Almond (1960). "A Functional Approach to Comparative Politics" in Gabriel A. Almond & James S. Coleman (Eds.). *The Politics of Developing Areas.* Princeton, N.J.: Princeton University Press. The Paperback edn., 1970, p. 47.
7. Gabriel A. Almond. *Ibid.*, p. 47.
8. David Easton (1965). (i) *A Framework for Political Analysis.* Englewood Cliffs, N. J: Prentice-Hall, p. 111, (ii) *A Systems Analysis of Political Life.* New York: John Wiley & Sons, 1965, pp. 29-33, 117-127, 411-429.
9. Lucian W. Pye (1963). "Introduction", in Lucian W. Pye (ed.), *Communications and Political Development* (Princeton, N.J.: Princeton University Press, Indian Reprint. New Delhi: Radha Krishna Prakashan, 1972, p. 6.
10. Jean Blondel (1969). *An Introduction to Comparative Government.* London: Weidenfeld & Nicholson, p. 223.
11. Jean Blondel, *Ibid.*, p. 223.
12. *Ibid.*
13. *Ibid.*
14. R.R. Fagen (1966). *Politics and Communication.* Boston: Little Brown & Co., p. 20.
15. R.B. Meadow (1960). *Politics as Communication.* Norwood, N.J.: Ablex Publishing Co., p. 4.
16. Ithiel de Sola Pool (1968). "Political Communication" in David L. Sills (ed), *International Encyclopaedia of the Social Sciences.* New York: MacMillan & the Free Press.
17. Karl W. Deutsch (1963). *The Nerves of Government—Models of Political Communication and Control.* New York: The Free Press, Vol. 3, pp. 90-95.
18. Karl W. Deutsch. *Ibid.*, pp. 118, 254.
19. *Ibid.*, p. 254.
20. *Ibid.*, p. 242.
21. *Ibid.*, pp. 152 & 254.
22. *Ibid.*, p. 124.
23. *Ibid.*, p. 145.
24. *Ibid.*, pp. 52, 254.
25. *Ibid.*, p. 152.
26. *Ibid.*, pp. 77-79.

27. *Ibid.*, p. 150.
28. *Ibid.*, p. 258.
29. *Ibid.*, pp. 27, 102.
30. *Ibid.*, p. 206.
31. *Ibid.*, pp. 118, 210.
32. *Ibid.*, pp. 80-81.
33. *Ibid.*, p. 88.
34. *Ibid.*
35. *Ibid.*, p. 192.
36. *Ibid.*, pp. 187, 188.
37. *Ibid.*, pp. 188, 189.
38. *Ibid.*, p. 164.
39. *Ibid.*
40. *Ibid.*
41. *Ibid.*, p. 16, 165, 195, 254.
42. Gabriel A. Almond. (i) "A Functional Approach to Comparative Politics" in Gabriel A. Almond & James S. Coleman (eds). *The Politics of Developing Areas. Op. cit.,* (ii) *Comparative Politics: A Developmental Approach*, authored with G.B. Powell, Jr. Boston: Little Brown & Company, 1966. Indian Reprint, New Delhi: Amerind Publishing Company, 1975.
43. Gabriel A. Almond. "A Functional Approach to Comparative Politics" in *the Politics of Developing Areas, Op. cit.*, p. 46.
44. Gabriel A. Almond. *Comparative Politics: A Developmental Approach, Op. cit.*, pp. 165-166.
45. Gabriel A. Almond. *Ibid.*, p. 167.
46. *Ibid.*, p. 170.
47. Gabriel A. Almond. *A Functional Approach to Comparative Politics, in the Politics of Developing Areas, Op. cit.,* p. 48.
48. Gabriel A. Almond. *Ibid.*, p. 49.
49. *Ibid.*, pp. 49-50.
50. *Ibid.*, p. 50.
51. Gabriel A. Almond. *Comparative Politics: A Developmental Approach, Op. cit.*, pp. 27-30.
52. Gabriel A. Almond *Ibid.*, p. 29.
53. *Ibid.*, p. 30.
54. *Ibid.*, p. 20.
55. *Ibid.*, p. 29.

8

Political Participation Theory

The analysis of Politics of a Society may be undertaken on the basis of the Theory of Political-Participation. Since the participation of the people in the Political Process of the Society enlivens and activates their political life, and thereby, there is commenced the dynamics of the Political System, it seems imperative to design and take the help of a theoretical framework for meaningful analysis of Politics both at the level of the individual and at the level of the Society. In this context, significant academic endeavours have been rendered by a number of eminent scholars including Lester E. Milbrath[1], Herbert Mc Closky[2], Robert E. Lane[3], S.M. Lipset[4], Sidney Verba[5], Norman H. Nie[6], Gabriel A. Almond[7] Carole Pateman[8], Angus Campbell[9], Samuel H. Barnes[10], and many others. All these scholarly contributions help-form relevant conceptual frameworks, what may be synthesized and be broadly termed as the Political-Participation Theory that may be meaningfully used by the researchers for analyzing and comprehending both Micro-Politics (Politics at the level of the individual) and Macro-Politics (Politics at the level of the Political System) in a Society.

The Concept of Political-Participation

The term "Political-Participation" connotes participatory activities undertaken by the individual and the people in the Political Process of a Society. As the political process encompasses the total process of "Authoritative allocation of values"[11] for the concerned Society, Political-Participation involves participatory activities undertaken in the process of (i) genesis of "values" or preferences on societal issues as ventilated in the form of demands, and their transmission to the Political Authority for making of authoritative decisions and policies, (ii) allocation of these demands, at the level of the Government or Political Authority, in the fotm of authoritative decisions; and (iii) effective implementation of these authoritative decisions on securing voluntary compliance of the people as well. Therefore, as Lester W. Milbrath[12] points out, all these activitie. by which people of a Society seek to influence or to support theii Government in the political process constitute the domain and scope of Political-Participation. Similarly, Herbert McClosky also opines that 'Political-Participation' consists of ''those voluntary activities by which members of a society share in the selection of rulers, and directly or indirectly in the formulation of public policy."[13] Thus, 'Political Participation' refers to those activities which people perform freely, without being forced or dictated, for electing their representatives who constitute the Government, and also for influencing the process of public policy-making as a whole. In this context, it may be noted that people may relate themselves to the Government and Politics in a variety of ways, and hence, 'Political-Participation' indeed, entails a wide variety of political and quasi-political activities[14] as, for instance, exposing one self to various political information and stimuli; listening to, and participating in discussions and debates on public and political affairs; making of demands for enactment of desired public policies; voting at the elections; conducting election campaigns; contesting at the elections; becoming members of Political Input-Structures such as Pressure-Groups and Political-Parties, and playing required roles; performing roles as incumbents of Political

Output-Structures such as Executive, Legislature and Judiciary; dissemination of politically relevant information through informal face-to-face contacts, traditional social-structures and groups, and through various specialized communication structures such as Mass-media; and also performing other related activities in the context of dynamics of the Political System. However, all these political-participatory activities, as Herbert McClosky[15] asserts, need to be allegiantly performed in the context of the dynamics of the Political System, and are expected to contribute towards its stability and viability. On the contrary, in the true lexical sense of the term, inimical participatory-activities, according to McClosky, do not come wider the rubric 'Political-Participation'. Hence, 'the Political-Participation Phenomenon' and the relevant participatory-activities seem to entail positive implications for the dynamics of the Political System. Of Course, the nature and type of participatory-activities may vary from individual to individual because every individual tends to relate himself to his Political System in a distinct and different way. Consequently, on the basis of varying degrees of interest in Politics and allegiance to the Political System, various forms of participatory-activities may be undertaken by the people of a Society. Hence, for the purpose of meaningful analysis, it seems imperative to classify these activities into some major types or forms.

A Typology of Political Participation

Following the conceptualization of Lester W. Milbrath[16], political-participatory activities may be classified into three major types or forms such as: (i) Gladiatorial-Activities, (ii) Transitional-Activities, and (iii) Spectator-Activities. These may be arranged in the following hierarchical order.

Types of Political-Participation

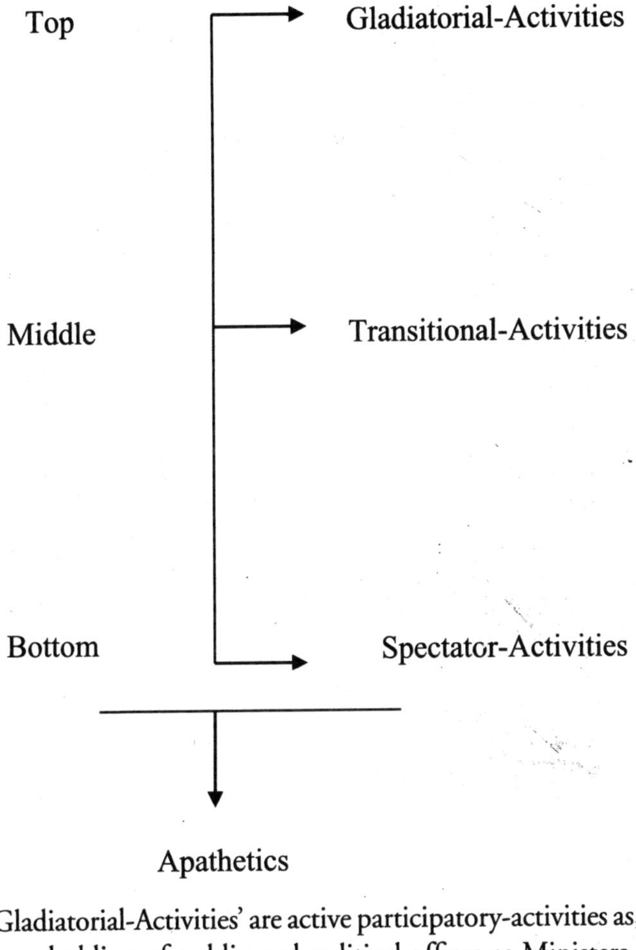

'Gladiatorial-Activities' are active participatory-activities as, for instance, holding of public and political offices as Ministers and Members of the Legislature; holding of Party offices as President and Members of its Executive Council, and playing roles in the decision-making process in these offices, and institutions; contesting the elections; and undertaking election campaigns etc. As distinguished from these activities characterized by intense involvement and active participation, 'Spectator-Activities' are characterized by minimal interest, and an extremely low-level of participation in Politics as, for instance, exposing one self to political information and stimuli; voting at the election simply; complying with the directions of the governmental officers, and also, of the political-party functionaries etc.

Thus, whereas 'Gladiatorial-Activities' occupy the top position in the hierarchical order of Types of Political-Participation, 'Spectator-Activities' occupy the bottom position. However, in between the top-position and the bottom-position in the hierarchical order, there may be placed the 'Transitional-Activities' characterized by an intermediate-level of interest and intensity of participation as, for instance, attending political and public meetings and rallies; maintaining contact with the political and party leaders; making monetary contribution to the party fund etc. Thus, 'Transitional-Participants' tend to be more interested and active than the Spectators but less active and involved in Politics than the Gladiators. Of course, this ordering of participatory-activities, as Milbrath[17] opines, indicates "a natural progression of being involved in politics", and hence, the Participants may involve themselves at different levels in playing participatory-activities and roles. Moreover, those persons who do not undertake any political participatory-activity, intentionally or unintentionally, and hence stand below the Spectators in the hierarchical order of participation may be termed as 'Apathetics.'[18]

Thus, 'Political-Participation Phenomenon' encompasses varieties of participatory activities of all Political Participants including the Gladiators, the Transitional Participants, and the Spectators even though wide variations may characterize their activities in respect of nature, extent, intensity, frequency, and scope of their participation. These variations in participatory-activities seem to originate from various factors such as the psychological needs and social characteristics of the participants, and also the peculiarities of the Political System as well. Hence, the major factors that tend to determine the pattern of 'Political-Participation' of an individual need to be discerned and analyzed.

Determinants of Political Participation

For discerning the Pattern of Political-Participation of an individual, and for undertaking a scientific analysis of it in the sense of finding out cause-effect relationship, it seems imperative to enquire into the question as to why he does participate and get himself involved in Politics. In this context, there may be discerned three major categories of determinants[19] such as: (i) Psychological Determinants, (ii) Social Determinants, and (iii) Political Determinants.

Psychological Determinants

Political-Participation, as Robert E. Lane[20] points out, may stem from the propensity of an individual to fulfil his psychological needs. These needs may be broadly classified, following the conceptualization of Abraham Harold Maslow[21], into five categories such as (i) physical needs pertaining to the maintenance and sustenance of the physical body; (ii) needs for safety pertaining to bodily-protection; (iii) needs for affection, (iv) needs for self-esteem and go-satisfaction; and (v) needs for self-actualization pertaining to the individual's higher self as a human being. The fulfilment of these needs may necessitate acquisition of vital societal-values such as wealth, power, status, recognition, prestige etc. These societal-values may be acquired by the individual through political-participation; and consequently, his needs may be gratified. However, for analyzing political-participatory activities of the individual as caused by motivations for gratification of his needs—material, social, and moral, it seems imperative to enquire into, and discern his personality-traits that tend to condition his psychology and pre-dispositions, because, as Herbet McClosky rightly opines, psychological needs of the individual stem from his "personality traits (whether primarily constitutional genetic or primarily leased."[22] In this context, the individual's personality may be classified as 'democratic personality'[23] if his psychology is characterized by democratic traits such as sociability or an instinct to be associated with fellow human beings and to share values with them; an Open-ego or an instinct for inter-personal trust that issues forth in a warm and inclusive attitude towards others; a sense of self-competence and efficacy; and an attitude of relative freedom from anxiety. These democratic-traits tend to induce the individual for 'Active Participation and Involvement' in Politics. This co-relationship between democratic traits and active political-participation has been investigated into and verified in a number of empirical studies; and hence, it may be hypothesized that individuals with democratic personality characterized by sociability, open ego, interpersonal trust, and sense of self competence are more likely to participate actively in Politics, and to play leading roles[24] than those with non-democratic personality. Moreover, as research evidences[25] indicate, individuals with democratic-personality tend to participate actively in Politics for fulfilment of higher level of psychological-need such as the need for self-actualization that emanates from a sense of civic obligation and humanness.

Thus, the individual's personality seems to condition his needs, and induces him to fix the priority among his materials needs, social needs, and moral needs to be realized through Political-Participation. He may participate in Politics for obtaining wealth, power, status and other material objectives. He may also participate in Politics for fulfilment of his social needs, and for overcoming his loneliness; and as Robert E. Lane points out: "Politics may offer to the lonely-man new opportunity for association with others—the excuse may be politics, the need may be fear of isolation."[26] Moreover, his very social life may create tensions or pain for him, and he may seek to diffuse or reduce such tensions through political participatory activities. Also, he may get himself involved in Politics for realization of his moral-needs that include self-actualization needs pertaining to his moral self, and also intellectual needs pertaining to his curiosity to know and understand the socio-political process. Thus, Political-Participation may be considered as an instrument or means through which the individual may strive to fulfil his various needs that stem from his psychology and personality. Of course, since these psychological variables are many and varied, and since these variables carry different relative weights, the assessment of their roles as determinants of Political-Participation seems to be a complex and difficult task.

Social Determinants

The Pattern of Political-Participation of the individual seems to be determined significantly by his social position in which he finds himself placed in the continua of various social variables. As Lester W. Milbrath emphatically states, the social-position variables "do form personalities, belief and attitudes which, in turns, do cause... participation in politics."[27] Of course, these social variables that accord distinct social positions to the individual and cause Political-Participation are many and varied; yet there may be discerned some major social variables such as Age, Gender, Race and Ethnicity, Income and Class, Occupation, Education, and Residence etc. that tend to influence, to a great extent, the participatory-activities and roles of the individual in the Political Process.

Age

The importance of Age a crucial determinant derives from the fact that Politics is considered as the domain of the adults probably because of the co-relationship between biological maturity and cognitive maturity of the individual.[28] Hence, only on attaining adulthood, the individual is allowed to exercise franchise in the electoral process, and also, to hold responsible positions in political and public institutions. As such, he gets opportunity to play effective political roles only during adulthood. It so happens probably because during the young-phase of adulthood, he tends to be the occupied mostly with the problems of searching for job or occupation; getting married and forming a family; whereas during the old-phase of adulthood, he tends to be increasingly pre-occupied with the problem of his prospective retirement from job or occupation, physical illness and inability, and also other worldly-worries. Therefore, in the middle-phase of adulthood, he is likely to be more active and involved in Politics than his young-adulthood, and old-adulthood.[29]

Gender

Gender or sex of the individual tends to determine the Pattern of his Political Participation as the Society is male-dominated, and Politics is also usually considered as the domain of the males. Consequently, the psychology and personality-traits of both males and females seem to be formed in different patterns during their infancy and childhood through the process of socialization undertaken by the Parents in the Family. Parents usually instruct, the male-child and the female-child to perform sex-appropriate roles[30] and they require the male-child to be most active in his interactions with others, and to play leadership roles; whereas they require the female-child to keep herself indoors, to help the mother in the kitchen, to be submissive and be concerned with her physical beauty, and to be indifferent to public affairs. Such differences in the Family's Socialization Process undertaken for the male-child and the female-child seem to form their psychology and personality in different forms; and consequently, the male-child tends to be more active and participant than the female-child in social life. As they grow up and become adults, they carry with them the attitudes and propensities learned already in the process of family's socialization, and tend to extend these to the political arena where they play political roles during adulthood. Therefore, in the sphere of Politics, males tend to be more informed, interested, active and efficacious than females.[31]

Income and Occupation

Income refers to the amount of money earned by the individual for his livelihood. It enables him not only to satisfy the material needs of life but also to live a life of comforts and leisure, free from material worries and anxieties. Simultaneously, it accords him a distinct status in the Society in relation to his fellow human-beings. Of course, the economic status of a human-being seems to be correlated with his occupation as income is earned through occupation. The individual, for earning his livelihood, engages himself in different types of occupations such as Agriculture, Business, and Profession. However, these occupations not only enable him to earn income for his livelihood but also tend to form his socio-economic status which, in turn, seems to determine the Pattern of his Political-Participation. Hence, it may be hypothesized that the higher is the level of his socio-economic status or class as determined by his income and occupation, the greater he may be active and involved in Politics.[32]

Education

Education broadens the mental horizon of the individual, develops his cognitive capacities, forms in him a sense of efficacy, and also, generates in him the curiosity to understand the total environment including the socio-political processes. As such, it makes him mentally active and participant, and simultaneously, accords him a distinct social status. Therefore, the educated individual tends to be informed, active, and efficacious in the socio-political processes. Hence, it may be hypothesized that the higher is the level of education of the individual, the greater may be his interest and participation in Politics.[33]

Ethnicity and Caste

Ethnicity and Caste are primordial identities that accord social-status to the individual in a traditional Society; and hence, these may serve as important social determinants of his participatory-activities in Politics.[34] It may, therefore, be hypothesized that higher is the ethnicity or caste of the individual, greater may be his participation in Politics. Of course, as the Traditional Society gradually modernizes itself, the social importance of ethnicity and caste tend to decline, but their political importance seems to increase at par with their political mobilization.

Residence

Residence or fixed abode may also serve as a social variable in influencing the political-participatory activities of the individual.[35] He may have his residence either in an urban area or a rural area; and it is his dwelling place that may help-form his social status. In this context, it may be noted that an urban-dweller, as compared to a rural-dweller, may have a higher socio-economic status because of greater opportunities for him for higher education, media exposure and information, professional occupation, and greater income. Hence, it may be hypothesized that the frequency and intensity of political-participation may be greater for an individual who resides in an urban area of the Society, and acquires an urban-economic status.

Thus, various social variables, traits, and identities, seem to determine conjointly the individual's Socio-Economic Status (SES) which, in turn, tends to influence significantly the Pattern of his Political-Participation. In this context, it may be hypothesized, on the whole, that the higher is the socio-economic status of the individual, the greater may be his involvement and participation in Politics.

Political Determinants

Political-Participation of the individual seems to be influenced by varieties of Political Determinants among which there may be discerned and analyzed some major factors or variables such as the Political System, Political Parties and Party System, Pressure Groups, National and International issues and crises, and the Individual's sense of Political Efficacy.[36]

The Political System

The Structure of the Political System through which authoritative decisions and policies are made and implemented may be classified into two major types such as: (i) the Open-Democratic Structure, and (ii) the Closed-Authoritarian Structure in terms of location and interplay of legitimate power within it. It is the structure of the Political System, whether Open-Democratic or Closed-Authoritarian, that tends to determine the Pattern of Political Participation of the people.[37] In the Open-Democratic Political System, legitimate power flows from the people to the Government which, as a consequence, becomes responsible and responsive to the former; whereas, in the closed-Authoritarian Political System, legitimate power remains concentrated in the Government which imposes its decisions upon the people without being responsible and responsive to them. Therefore, the Open-Democratic Political System, as distinguished from the Closed-Authoritarian Political System, provides for free flow of political information; and for freedom of expression of demands, freedom for political assembly and association, freedom for exercising franchise, and freedom for contesting elections and holding political offices. Hence, the Open-Democratic Political System, on providing motivations and structural opportunities to the people for effective and meaningful political-participation, tends to influence the nature and frequency of their political-participatory activities.

Moreover, Political-Participation of the individual seems to be influenced by the nature of the Rules of the Game[38] of Politics in a Society. These rules are codified as Provisions of the Constitution that seek to regulate and control not only the political process out also the activities and behaviour of all political actors including the primary citizens, and the incumbents of various political and public institutions. However, the Provisions of the Constitution, and the Laws and Rules of the Political Game seem to facilitate active Political Participation and Involvement for the people provided these are simple and easily comprehensible to the people at large; whereas complicated and incomprehensible Constitutional Provisions and Rules tend to affect adversely the nature and frequency of Political-Participation of the citizens.

Political Parties and the Party System

Political-Parties are the inevitable agencies for formation of Government in the Democratic Polity. They compete with one another in the electoral battle for obtaining people's mandate for forming the Government. However, for political and electoral competition to take place, there must emerge in the Society either the Multi-Party System or (at the minimum) the Bi-Party-System. Moreover, for becoming successful in these political and electoral competitions, Political Parties seek to obtain support and allegiance of the people, and for this purpose, they organize public meetings, distribute leaflets and manifestoes, conduct political campaigns, and undertake political education of the people through various measures and methods. All these activities of Political-Parties, and their inter-party competitions not only provide political information to the people but also help-create political interest in them for active and effective Political-Participation.[39]

Pressure-Groups

Pressure-Groups are non-political social groups that represent homogenous interests of different sections of population, and seek to exert pressure upon the Government for protecting and promoting their articulated-objectives. Even though they are characterized by non-political objectives, they perform quasi-political activities, and hence, they may serve as vital political-determinants in influencing the Pattern of Political-Participation of their respective members.[40] They tend to make their members active in devising channels of access to the decision-making centre in the Government, and in exerting influence upon the Political Decision-Makers for realizing their objectives. As such, the activities of the Pressure-Groups seem to create a congenial mindset for their members respectively for active participation and involvement in Politics.

Public Issues and Crises

Awareness of the individual on emerging National and International Issues and Crises may determine the Pattern of his Political-Participation.[41] As and when he becomes aware of pressing National Issues, for instance, issues of Human Rights, Civil Liberty, Social Justice, Liberalization or Nationalization of Economy, Educational and Health-Care facilities etc., may form in him high political interest which, in turn, may motivate him to seek redressal through Political-Participation.

Sense of Political Efficacy or Competence

The Sense of Political-Efficacy or Competence refers to the belief and confidence of the individual in himself that he can influence the Government and the policy-making process successfully. Accordingly, he may work through various institutional means and channels, for instance Political-Parties, Mass-media including television, radio, news-papers, journals etc. He may even work individually on petitioning the Government, and filling Public Interest Litigation Case in the Judiciary. While undertaking these peaceful activities in protest against public policies, laws, rules and regulations that he considers unjust, and hence, he demands remedies or amendments, he remains unconcerned as to the extent of actual success in goal attainment. It is this subjective Sense of Political-Efficacy or Competence which motivates him for active Political-Participation. Therefore, the Pattern of Political-Participation of the individual seems to be greatly correlated with his subjective Sense of Political-Efficiacy.[42]

Conjoint Impact of the Determinants

Thus, there may be discerned varieties of psychological, social and political variables and correlates of Political-Participation. However, these determinants do not function in isolation to one another, but tend to determine conjointly the Pattern of Political-Participation of the individual. Of course, since the determinants are so many and varied with different relative weights, and since the co-relationships between them and the individual's participatory-activities are so complex and intricate, the accurate discernment and exact measurement of their impact seem to be an arduous task. Hence, rigorous research endeavours are required for ascertaining them, and also, the extent of their impact.

Political-Participation and the Political System

Political-Participation infuses dynamism into the Political System, and enlivens it. As and when members of a Society perform allegiantly-participatory roles in the context of formation of

Inputs (Demands and Support), and Outputs (Authoritative decisions), and render allegiance to it, the Political System having been endowed with legitimacy becomes a dynamic entity, and it tends to function with stability and viability. Therefore, 'Allegiant Political-Participation' seems to be the life-force of every Polity irrespective of the fact as to whether it is large or small in size; and authoritarian or democratic in ideology and structure. In the case of an Authoritarian-Polity where freedom for Political-Participation does not exist, and the scope and domain of Political-Participation become extremely limited and directed, its Ruler (the Government) even invariably tries to clothe his arbitrary decisions with the veil of a mass approval secured through some form of Political-Participation of its people. As distinguished from it, a Democratic-Polity seeks to secure legitimacy from the people, manifestly and directly, on providing them opportunities for open, free and universal Political-Participation. In this context, Herbert McClosky emphatically points out: "Participation is the principal means by which consent is granted or withdrawn in a democracy, and rulers are made accountable to the ruled."[43] Moreover, free and universal Political-Participation may provide opportunity to the Government to be benefitted by the wisdom and experiences of the people in the matter of policy-making and governance. Simultaneously, it may help-check the self-aggrandizing and unscrupulous tendencies of the Government, and may make the latter responsive and responsible to the people. Hence, in a Democracy, as Herbert McClosky asserts, "participation is power"[44]; and as Gabriel A. Almond and Sidney Verba opine: "citizen competence and participation are at the heart of democracy."[45]

Thus, on contributing towards legitimacy, stability, and viability of the Polity, and making the Government responsible and responsive to 'the Governed', 'Political Participation' seems to facilitate, and promote the process of Development of the National Political System. Scope and opportunities for free and universal Political-Participation may create and foster in the people a sense of loyalty and belongingness towards the Political System, and hence, may contribute towards formation as well as reinforcement of their national identity which stands out as the first prerequisite for Political Development. Therefore, as regards the overall relevance of 'Political-Participation' for the Political System, Lucian W. Pye emphatically points out: "Political development does entail some degree of extended participation ...participation has a role to play in nation-building activities since it represents a means of creating loyalties and a new feeling of national identity."[46]

A Critical Appraisal

The Political Participation Theory, on emphasizing on 'Allegiance' of the people in the context of performance of their roles and activities in the 'Political Process of a Society', seems to present a rosy and visionary image of its political stability and development. Theoretically, it seems to be well-indicated and linked. However, when it is examined and analyzed in empirical situation, it may be found to be superfluous and unattainable in most of the Societies of the world. Its shortcoming may be traced to the absence of 'Equal Liberty' which is the most essential prerequisite for effective and equal 'Political Participation' of all citizens in the political process of a Society. The Constitution of a Democratic-Polity, no doubt, provides for the provision of equal political liberty for all its citizens, but in reality, 'Liberty without Socio-Economic Equality' becomes a myth for them. Since every Society is characterized by endemic and widespread socio-economic inequalities among its people, and hence, since there is absence of effective liberty for them, people's Political-Participation cannot become truly effective and meaningful. As a consequence, the extent of 'Effective Political-Participation' may remain limited to a few individuals (the Elites) who possess the vital resources of the Society, and who, as such, are capable of exercising influence and power over the majority of people. Moreover, since effective 'Political-Participation' tends to be limited to a few Elites, most of the people of the Society remain discontented, and hence alienated to the Political System. Such an emerging sense of political-apathy and alienation may generate revolt and anti-national activities which would create stupendous hindrances for attainment of socio-political stability and political development of a National Society.

Hence, every National Society, through its Political System, needs to undertake measures for bringing about widespread socio-economic equality among its people, and for providing them equality of opportunities and true 'Equality of Liberty' so that its people, as a whole, may be enabled to participate effectively, meaningfully, and that too, allegiantly in its political process. Consequently, there may be ensured its political stability and a higher level of political-development.

Notes

1. Lester W. Milbrath (1965). *Political Participation: How and Why Do people Get Enveloped in Politics*. Chicago: Rand McNally & Company.
2. Herbert McClosky (1968). "Political Participation" in David & Sills (ed.), *International Encyclopedia of the Social Science*. New York: Collier-MacMillan, Vol. 2.
3. Robert E. Lane (1959). *Political Life: Why People Get Involved in Politics*. New York: Free Press.
4. S.M. Lipset. *Political Man: Social Bases of Politics*. New York: Garden City: Double Day, 1900.
5. Sidney Verba (1972). *Political Participation in America: Political Democracy and Social Equality*. New York: Harper & Row, authored in collabouration with Norman H. Nie.
6. Nooran H. Nie. *Ibid.*, authored in collabouration with Sidney Verba.
7. Gabriel A. Almond (1963). *The Civic Culture: Political Attitudes and Democracy in Five Nations*. Princeton, N.J.: Princeton University Press. Authored in collabouration with Sidney Verba.
8. Carole Pateman (1970). *Participation and Democratic Theory*. London: Cambridge University Press.
9. Angus Campbell *et al.* (1960). *The American Voter*. New York: Wiley.
10. Samuel H. Barnes, *et al.* (1979). *Political Action: Mass Participation in Five Western Democracies*. Beverly Hills, California: Sage Publications.
11. David Easton (1953), *Political System: An Enquiry into the State of Political Science*. New York: Alfred Knopf. Indian Reprint, Calcutta: Scientific Book Company, 1971, p. 129.

12. Lester W. Milbrath & M.L. Goel. (1977). *Political Participation.* Chicago: Rand McNally Publishing Co., 2nd edn., p. 2.
13. Herbert McClosky (1968). "Political Participation" in David L. Sills (ed.), *International Encyclopedia of the Social Science.* New York, Collier MacMillion, Vol. 12, p. 252.
14. Herbert McClosky. *Ibid.*, p. 252. See, also, Lester W. Milbrath & M. L. Goel. *Political Participation, Op. cit.*, pp. 8-11.
15. Herbert McClosky. *Political Participation. Op. cit.*, p. 252.
16. Lester W. Milbrath (1965). *Political Participation.* Chicago: Rand McNally Publishing Co., p. 18.
17. *Ibid.*, p. 19.
18. Lester W. Milbrath & M.L. Goel. *Political Participation, Op. cit.*, p. 21.
19. Herbert McClosky. *Political Participation. Op. cit.*, p. 256.
20. Robert E. Lane (1959). *Political Life—Why People get Involved in Politics.* New York: Free Press, pp. 101-111.
21. Abraham Harold Maslow (1954): *Motivation and Personality.* New York: Harpin.
22. Herbert McClosky. *Political Participation. Op. cit.*, p. 258.
23. Harold D. Lasswell (1946). *Power and Personality.* New York, p. 148. *The Political Writings of Harold D. Lasswell.* Glencoe, Illinois, 1951, p. 495.
24. (i) Lester W. Milbrath & Walter Klein (1962). "Personality Correlates of Political Participation", *Acta Sociologica* 6 (fasc.1-2), pp. 53-66. (ii) Robert E. Lane (1959). *Political Life—Why People Get Involved in Politics.* Glencoe, Illinois: The Free Press. (iii) James C. Davies (1963). *Human Nature on Politics.* New York: Wiley, pp. 34-36. (iv) Yasamasa Kuroda (1965), "Sociability and Political Involvement", *Midwest Journal of Political Science*, 9, pp. 133-147. (v) Pearl Mayo Gore & Julian B. Rotter (1963), "A Personality Correlate of Social Action", *Journal of Personality* 341, pp. 58-64. (vi) Rodenik Bell (1969). "The Determinants of Psychological Involvement in Politics—A Causal Analysis", *Midwest Journal of Political Science, 3*, pp. 237-253. (vii) Fred, I. Greenstein (1969), *Personality and Politics—Problems of Evidence, Inference, and Conceptualization.* Chicago: Markham, Publishing Co. (viii) Sheldon G. Levy (1970). "The Psychology of Political Activity", *Annals of Political Science*, 391, pp. 83-96. (ix) Fred, I, Greenstein & Michael Lerner (eds) (1971). *A Source Book for the Study of Personality and Politics.* Chicago: Markham, Publishing & Co. (x) Jeane Nickel Knertson (1972). *The Human Basis of the*

Polity—A Psychological Study of Political Man. Chicago: Aldine-Atherton. (xi) Stanley Allen Renshon (1974). *Psychological Needs and Political Behaviour—A Theory of Personality and Political Efficacy*. New York: The Free Press. (xii) Paul M. Sniderman (1975). *Personality and Democratic Politics*. (Berkeley: University of California Press.

25. (i) Angus Campbell Geraid Gurin and Warren E. Miller (1954). *The Voter Decides*. Evanston, Illinois: Row, Peterson. (ii) Angus Campbell, Phillip E. Converse, Warren Miller, and Donald Stokes (1960). *The American Voter*. (New York: Wiley. (iii) Christian Bay (1968). "Needs, Wants, and Political Legitimacy", *Canadian Journal of Political Science*, pp. 241-260. (iv) Robert E. Lane (1969). *Political Thinking and Consciousness: The Private Life of the Political Mind*, Chicago Markham, Publishing Co. (v) Jeanne Nickel Knutson (1972). *The Human Basis of the Polity—A Psychological Study of Political Man*. Chicago: Aldine-Atherton.
26. Robert Elane (1961). *Political Life—Why People Get Involved in Politics*. Glencoe, Illinois: The Free Press, p. 108.
27. Lester W. Milbrath & M.L. Goel. *Political Participation: How and Why do People Get Involved in Politics, Op. cit.*, p. 86.
28. Lawrence G. Kohlberg (1969). "Stage and Sequence—The Cognitive Development Approach to Socialization" in David Goslin (ed), *Handbook of Socialization: Theory and Research*. Chicago: Rand McNally & Co., pp. 347-380.
29. (i) N.E. Cutler (1974). "Aging and Generations in Politics", in A.R. Wilcox (ed), *Public Opinion and Political Attitudes: A Reader*. New York: Wiley. (ii) Robert E. Lane (1959). *Political Life: Why People Get involved in Politics*. Glencoe Illinois: The Free Press. (iii) S.M. Lipset (1960). *Political Man: Social Bases of Politics*. New York, Garden City: Double Day. (iv) Sidney Verba & Norman H. Nie (1972). *Participation in America: Political Democracy and Social Equality*. New York: Harper & Row. (v) M.L. Goel (1975). *Political Participation in a Developing Nation: India*. New York: Asia Publishing House.
30. (i) Fred, I. Greenstein (1965). *Children and Politics*. New Haven: Yale University Press, pp. 115-118. (ii) Robert E. Dowse & John A. Hughes (March, 1971). "Girls, Boys, and Politics", *British Journal of Sociology*, 22, pp. 53-67.
31. (i) Gabriel A. Almond & Sidney Verba (1963). *The Civics Culture—Political Attitudes and Democracy in Five Nations*. Princeton, N.J., Princeton University Press. (ii) Lester W. Milbrath & M.L. Goel. *Political Participation, Op. cit.*, p. 116.

32. (i) Robert A. Dahl (1961). *Who Governs? Democracy and Power in an American City*. New Haven: Yale University Press. (ii) Norman H. Nie, G.B. Powell, Jr. and Kenneth Prewitt (1969). "Social Structure & Political Participation: Developmental Relationship", Part-I & II, *American Political Science Review*, 63, pp. 361-78, 808-32. (iii) Sidney Verba & Norman H. Nie (1972). *Participation in American Political Democracy and Social Equality*. New York: Harper & Row.
33. (i) Gabriel A. Almond & Sidney Verba (1963). *The Civics Culture—Political Attitudes and Democracy in Five Nations*. Princeton, N.J.: Princeton University Press, especially, Chapter 3, 4, 7, 9, 10 and 11. (ii) Sidney Verba & Norman H. Nie (1972). *Participation in American Political Democracy and Social Equality*. New York: Harper & Row.
34. (i) Angus Campbell, Gerald Gurin and Warren B. Miller (1954). *The Voter Decides*. Evanston, Illinois: Row, Peterson. (ii) Sidney Verba & Norman H. Nie (1972). *Participation in American Political Democracy and Social Equality*. New York: Harper & Row.
35. (i) Stein Rokkan & Angus Campbell (1960). "Norway and United States of America" in *Citizen Participation in Political Life, International Social Science Journal*, 2, pp. 69-99. (ii) William N. McPhee & William A. Glaser (eds) (1962). *Public Opinion and Congressional Elections*. New York: The Free Press of Glencoe.
36. Herbert McClosky. *Political Participation, Op. cit.*, pp. 259-262.
37. Lester W. Milbrath & M.L. Goel. *Political Participation: How and Why do People Get Involved in Politics, Op. cit.* pp. 144-155.
38. Lester W. Milbrath (1971). "Individuals and the Government" in Herber-Jacob and Kenneth N. Vines (eds), *Politics in the American States: A Comparative Analysis*. Boston: Little, Brown & Co, pp. 27-81.
39. (i) Robert E. Agge, Daniel Goldrich, and Bert E. Swanson (1964). *The Rulers and the Ruled*. New York: Wiley. (ii) Lester W. Milbrath (1965). "Political Participation in the States" in Herber-Jacob and Kenneth N. Vines (eds), *Politics in the American States: A Comparative Analysis*. Boston: Little, Brown & Co.
40. Robert E. Lane (1959). *Political Life: Why People Get Involved in Politics*. Glencoe, Illinois: The Free Press.
41. Herbert McClosky. "Political Participation" *Op. cit.*, pp. 261-262.
42. (i) Gabriel A. Almond & Sidney Verba (1963). *The Civics Culture: Political Attitudes and Democracy in Five Nations*. Princeton, N.J., Princeton University Press. (ii) Lester W. Milbrath & M.L. Goel. *Political Participation, Op. cit.*, p. 56. (iii) Carole Pateman (1970).

Participation and Democratic Theory. London: Cambridge University Press, p. 46.

43. Herbert McClosky. *Political Participation. Op. cit.*, p. 253.
44. Herbert McClosky (1972). *Ibid.*, p. 263.
45. Gabriel A. Almond & Sidney Verba. *The Civic Culture: Political Attitudes and Democracy in Five Nations*. Princeton, N.J., Princeton University Press, 4th Printing, p. 230.
46. Lucian W. Pye. *Aspects of Political Development*. Boston: Little Brown & Co, 1965, pp. 39-42.

9

Political Development Theory

The overall dynamics of the Political System of a National Society reveals the level of its development. Simultaneously, the level of its 'Political Development' tends to accord it a distinct status in the community of the Nation-States of the world. Hence, it becomes imperative to assess and ascertain the level of its 'Political Development'. For this purpose, scholarly endeavours have been undertaken in designing relevant conceptual frameworks which may be captioned as 'The Theory of Political-Development'.

The Concept of Political Development

The nomenclature 'Political Development' seems to connote, broadly, the level of development of Politics of a National Society. Since, the Politics of a Society involves the entire process of 'authoritative allocation of values'[1] for it as undertaken by its Political System, the term 'Political Development' connotes specifically the level of development of the concerned Political System. Hence, it must not be comprehended as synonymous with such terms as 'the Process of Political Evolution' or 'History of Political Events'; rather it needs to be understood as the indices or features and attributes of development that characterize the Society's Political System. In this context of identification and delineation of the indices of 'Political Development', many significant contributions are found to have been rendered by a large number of scholars among whom some prominent theorists are: Lucian W. Pye[2], James S. Coleman[3], Myron Weiner[4], Joseph LaPalombara[5], Leonard Binder[6], Samuel P. Huntington[7], Paul A. Baran[8], Benjamin Higgins[9], David E. Apter[10], Walt W. Rustow[11], S.M. Lipset[12], K.H. Silvert[13], Clifford Geertz[14], Rupert Emerson[15], Karl W. Deutsch[16], Fred W. Riggs[17], Max F. Millikan[18] and Daniel Larner.[19] Their scholarly contributions that focus on the essential features of Political Development are different and divergent. However, despite prevalence of semantic differences, and lack of consensus on a common-accepted set of features, an endeavour in grouping compatible conceptualizations into ten broad categories has been undertaken by Lucian W. Pye.[20] It would facilitate the process of meaningful scrutiny and analysis of the 'Political Development Phenomenon'.

Divergent Perspectives on Political Development Phenomenon

Lucian W. Pye classifies the prevalent perspectives and conceptualizations on the 'Political Development Phenomenon' into ten broad categories[21]; these are: (1) Political Development as the Political Prerequisite of Economic Development, (2) Political Development as the Politics Typical of Industrial Societies, (3) Political Development as Political Modernization, (4) Political Development as the operation of a Nation-State, (5) Political Development as Administrative and Legal Development, (6) Political Development as Mass-mobilization and Participation, (7) Political Development as Building of Democracy, (8) Political Development as Stability and Orderly-Change, (9) Political Development as Mobilization and Power, (10) Political Development as one Aspect of a Multidimensional Process of Social Change.

Political Development as the Political Prerequisite of Economic Development

This perspective that portrays the phenomenon of Political Development as the Political Prerequisite of Economic Development is presented by some scholars such as Paul A. Baran[22], Norman S. Buchanan[23], Benjamin Higgins[24], and Barbara Ward.[25] According to these scholars, Political Development would take place only when the concerned Society becomes economically developed. For them, economic development is indicated by people's attainment of high per-capita income which, in turn, creates conducive conditions for social stability and facilitates the Society's Political Development.

Political Development as the Politics Typical of Industrial Societies

This perspective considers Political Development as synonymous with the Politics or the Pattern of Political Order that prevails in an Industrial Society. It is presented by some scholars among whom the pioneer is Walt W. Rostow.[26] The assumption of this perspective is that every industrial society characterized by high industrial growth produces a more or less common type of political life with common standards of political behaviour and performance such as rational and responsible governmental behaviour, appreciation of the values of orderly administrative and legal procedure, and people's acknowledgement that Politics is a mechanism for solving societal problems, not an end in itself. These political attributes which emerge in an industrial society are considered to be the distinguishing features of Political Development.

Political Development as Political Modernization

This perspective that presents Political Development as Political Modernization is the view of some scholars such as David E. Apter[27], James S. Coleman[28], Seymour Martin Lipset[29], and Karl W. Deutsch.[30] According to these scholars, Political Modernization is characterized by some salient attributes such as prevalence of universal secular laws, merit system of recruitment to public offices, formation of differentiated political input infrastructures including pressure groups, political parties, and mass-media, the practice of active citizenship, prevalence of justice and rationality in administration. These attributes make for Political Development in a Society.

Political Development as the Operation of a Nation-State

The perspective that postulates Political Development as the Operation of a Nation-State is the view of some scholars such as K.H. Silvert[31], Edward Shils[32], and William Mc Cord.[33] The assumption of this perspective is that the emergence of a Nation-State produces Nationalism which is the hallmark of Political Development of a Society. For the emergences of a Nation-State, the prerequisite are: (i) State-building involving the building of the political infrastructures such as mass-media, pressure groups, and political parties in addition to the governmental structures such as legislature, executive and judiciary; and (ii) emotional integration of the people with the National Society on acquiring a high sense of Nationalism. Consequently, the emergence of a Nation-State and its successful operation would make it politically developed as it helps-form a capacity to maintain a high level of public order, to mobilize resources for public enterprises, and to uphold international commitments.

Political Development as Administrative and Legal Development

This notion of Political Development is presented by scholars such as Max Weber[34] and Joseph LaPalombara.[35] According to these scholars, Political Development of a Society is characterized by some essential features such as formation of a rational and effective bureaucracy with technical and specialized knowledge to solve societal problems; management of public affairs effectively by a competent and efficient administrative system; and the prevalence of a rational, secular, and universal legal code.

Political Development as Mass-Mobilization and Participation

This perspective is presented by scholars such as Clifford Geertz[36], Rupert Emerson[37] and Bert F. Hoselitz.[38] According to these scholars, Political Development necessarily involves participant roles of the citizenry with loyalty and allegiance to the State. Hence, the citizens must be mass-mobilized to participate actively and allegiantly in the societal political process. People's Political Mobilization would instil in them a sense of belongingness to the Nation-State, and consequently, their allegiant participation would help produce political order and stability in the Society. As such, Political Development is essentially characterized by the prevalence of Mass-Mobilization and Participation of the Citizens in Politics.

Political Development as the Building of Democracy

The perspective that Political Development is the Building of Democracy is presented by some scholars among whom Joseph LaPalombara[39] is a pioneer. This perspective assumes that Political Development in a Society cannot take place unless democratic institutions are built, and democratic principles are truly followed and practiced. For this purpose, there must be established a responsible and responsive Government which is based on the consent of the people as expressed through periodic elections, and there must prevail a free and fair electoral system that conducts elections through which people elect their representatives to form the Government, a Constitutional System that upholds the rule of law, and that provides for equal political liberty to all citizens on upholding the principles of universal adult franchise, and also, there must be guaranteed fundamental rights to the citizens.

Political Development as Stability and Orderly Change

Some scholars such as Karl W. Deutsch[40] and Fred W. Riggs[41] consider Political Development as the Political System's capability for maintaining stability and bringing about orderly change. The basic assumption of this perspective is that a Political System cannot attain the developed status unless and until the Society achieves a high level of socio-economic development which, of course, becomes possible only when there is established durable political stability. However, political stability does not mean merely the maintenance of socio-political status-quo because change must occur in every Political Society in conformity with the changes in the socio-economic political environment, and also, with the emergence of new ideas and ideologies. Hence, political stability may be attained provided the Political System possesses the required capacity to control and direct societal changes purposefully for achieving the desired goals while maintaining itself.

Political Development as Mobilization and Power

This perspective that considers Political Development as Mobilization and Power is presented by some scholars such as James S. Coleman[42], Gabriel A. Almond[43], and S.N. Eisenstadt.[44] The basic assumption of this perspective is that power is the most distinguishing hallmark of a Political System because it is essentially concerned with the making of authoritative public policies for the Society as a whole, and of implementing these effectively. For this purpose, it requires to possess and also, to use legitimate power. Therefore, a Political System may attain the developed status provided it is powerful enough to make and implement public policies effectively. However, for possessing effective power, the Political System needs to acquire a high level of people's legitimacy on mobilizing their willing and spontaneous support towards it. Hence, possession of a high level of Mobilization-Capacity may enable the Political System to become powerful enough to achieve wider range of common goals of the people through implementation of welfare-oriented public policies; and consequently, it would be enabled to attain stability and development.

Political Development as One Aspect of a Multidimensional Process of Social Change

This perspective is presented by some scholars such as Max F. Millikan[45], and Daniel Lerner[46] who consider that Political

Development is only one dimension of the totality of societal transformation and change. The basic assumption of this view is that Society is a composite of varieties of Systems such as the Social System, the Economic System, the Political System, the Ecological System etc. Because the Political System as an integral part of the Society, it would automatically develop when the Society, as a whole, including all its Systems gets developed and modernized. Societal-Modernization simultaneously generates modernizing tendencies in the Political System, and helps-form modern and developed attributes in it. Accordingly, Political Development is viewed as One Aspect of a Multidimensional Process of Societal Change that takes place in the context of its modernization.

Need for a Comprehensive and Coherent Theory of Political Development

All these above perspectives and conceptualizations on the Political Development Phenomenon are found to be inchoate and incoherent because each of these identify and elucidate only one or a few attributes, and that too, differently and divergently. Since none of these perspectives is found to be coherent and comprehensive in itself to characterize and portray the level of Political Development of a Political System in its totality, there is felt the necessity to design a Comprehensive and Coherent Theory of Political Development in order to minimize and settle the semantic confusions and disagreements on the concept of Political Development. Hence, for analyzing the Political Development Phenomenon empirically, meaningfully, and systematically, there was undertaken a path-breaking academic endeavour[47], in 1963, by the Comparative Politics Committee of the Social Science Research Council of USA. This Committee was composed of a number of distinguished Political Scientists among whom some noteworthy scholars are Lucian W. Pye, Leonard Binder, James S. Coleman, Joseph LaPalombara, Myron Weiner, and Sidney Verba. This group of eminent Political Scientists, through insightful academic discussions and interactions, designed a Comprehensive and Coherent Theory of Political Development, what is famously known as the "Development Syndrome"[48], in order to enquire into and ascertain empirically the level of Political-Development of a Nation-State, and also to undertake a meaningful comparative analysis of all the Nation-States of this world in respect of the Political-Development Phenomenon.

The Development-Syndrome: Parameters and Indices

'The Political-Development Syndrome' comprises of three major Parameters (Dimensions)[49] of the scale for measuring the level Development of a Political System; and these parameters are: (i) Equality, (ii) Capacity, and (iii) Differentiation. These three Parameters are interrelated, and conjointly, these may constitute the referral variables for enquiring into the three dimensions such as Equality, Capacity, and Differentiation of the Political System in order to measure and ascertain the level of its Development.

The Parameter of Equality

The parameter of 'Equality' consists of three variables[50] such as: (i) the Political-Participation System, (ii) the Legal-System and (iii) the Public-Recruitment System. These three variables are to be enquired into in the context of the dynamics of a National Political Society. As regards the Political-Participation System, investigation may be made in respect of the Nature, the Extent, and the Scope of people's participation in the political process of the Society. In this context, the Indices of Development are mass-participation, and popular involvement in the political process. It is required that people are to participate in large number, and that too extensively and actively in the political process. Such mass-participation and active involvement of the people in all arenas of socio-political life may take place provided the Political System offers constitutional guarantees for political equality and freedom of political-participation. Accordingly, there must be provided to the people a set of fundamental rights and liberty so as to enable them to participate actively and spontaneously in the political process by way of ventilating their demands, grievances, and choices through the Input-institutions such as Mass-media, Pressure-Groups, Political-Parties, and the Governmental Institutions such as the Electoral System. Thus, as regards the variable of the Political-Participation System, the attributes of development are Mass-Participation and Active-Involvement of the people in the Society's Political Process.

As regards the Legal-System, the Indices of Development are Rationalism, Secularism, and Universalism of the Laws which are enacted and enforced in the Political Society. The laws need to be founded on (i) Right Reason (Rationalism) that champions human values and objective-goodness, (ii) Secularism that champions temporal (this worldly) values as against religious values, and (iii) Universalism that champions the principles of Equality before Law and Rule of Law. These attributes, on being manifested in the Legal-System, would make it a developed one.

As regards the Public-Recruitment System, the Indices of Development are Merit and Achievement as against ascription and patronage. It is required that the recruitment to public offices must be made on the basis of merit and achievement of the candidates as adjudged through open competitive examinations or selection procedure, not on ascriptive considerations of status, wealth, inheritance or heritage of the candidates, or patronage and recommendation made by some powerful mentors and persons. Hence, the Public-Recruitment System may attain the developed status provided it becomes achievement-oriented and merit-based.

Thus, each of these three variables of the parameter of Equality is characterized by distinct Indices of Development. The Political-Participation System may be adjudged as a developed one provided it is characterized by mass-participation and active-involvement of the people in the socio-political process; the Legal-System may be adjudged as a developed one provided it is characterized by the attributes of rationalism, secularism, and universalism; and the Public-Recruitment System may be adjudged as a developed one provided it is merit and achievement-based. These three variables of the parameter of Equality, of course, are to be evaluated conjointly with reference to the indices of development, and accordingly, the level of Equality in a Political Society may be ascertained in the Development Scale.

The Parameter of Capacity

The parameter of Capacity or Capability constitutes the second major parameter in respect of which the level of Development of a Political System may be measured and ascertained. It connotes the Political System's effectiveness and efficiency in the execution of public policies. It is an essential parameter because a Developed Political System is expected not only to make and execute more public policies than other systems but also to do faster, and with much greater thoroughness, rationality, and professionalization.[51] It, thus, involves the overall performance of a Political System as a distinct unit in the environment in the context of successful attainment of the societal goals and objectives. Empirically, it may be enquired into, and measured, as Gabriel A. Almond[52] also succinctly proposes, in respect of four dimensions of the Systemic-Capability such as: (i) the Extractive capability, (ii) the Regulative Capability, (iii) the Distributive Capability, and (iv) the Responsive Capability.

The Extractive Capability refers to the capability of a Political System to extract resources including goods and services from its people in the form of taxes and personnel for discharging its public functions. It is essential for the Political System to extract taxes and services from the people because money and personnel are basically required for making it functionally viable and stronger in reality. Hence, the greater is its Extractive Capability, the greater may be the level of its performance and development.

The Regulative Capability refers to the capability of a Political System to regulate people's behaviour and activities. Effective regulation of people's behaviour through punitive actions for violating laws becomes necessary for maintenance of peace, order, and stability in the Political Society. Hence, the greater is the Regulative Capacity of a Political System, the greater may be the level of its performance and development.

The Distributive Capability refers to the capability of a Political System to distribute goods and services among its people for their overall benefit and welfare. The Political System has come into existence, and it continues to exist for the good of the people, and as such, it is expected by the people to deliver benefits and advantages to them. Hence, the greater is the Distributive Capability of a Political System, the greater may be the level of its performance and development.

The Responsive Capability refers to the capability of a Political System to respond actively and positively to people's opinions and demands. The Political System is expected to be responsible to the people for all its acts of omission and commission, and simultaneously, to be responsive to the vox-populi (People's Opinions). Its responsiveness would generate and foster a high sense of belonging in the people towards it. Consequently, on acquiring people's support and legitimacy, the Political System would be enabled to function with greater stability and viability. Moreover, a high level of Responsive Capability would, most likely, enable the Political System to display higher Extractive, Regulative, and Distributive Capabilities because people's allegiant support would entail their willing and spontaneous payment of taxes and levies, and obedience to the laws and regulations; and simultaneously, the Political System would be enabled for undertaking needful distribution of societal resources through welfare public policies.

Hence, the higher is the level of the overall Systemic-Capability or Capacity of a Political System including its Extractive Capability, Regulative capability, Distributive capacity and Responsive capability, the greater may be the level of its performance and development.

The Parameter of Differentiation

The parameter of Differentiation is the third major parameter of Political Development. For this purpose, Differentiation connotes

'Structural-Differentiation' accompanied with Functional-Specificity and Specialization in the context of 'Structural-Functional Relationship'[53] in a Political System. In order to become dynamic, the Political System is required to perform, as Gabriel A. Almond[54] postulates, seven major types of Functions which include four types of Input-Functions such as the Function of Political Socialization, the Function of Political Communication, the Function of Interest-Articulation, the Function of Interest-Aggregation; and three types of Output-Functions such as the Function of Rule-Making, the Function of Rule-Application, and the Function of Rule-Adjudication. For performing these Functions meaningfully, it is required that relevant Structures corresponding to each of these Functions must be formed, and that each Structure must perform its corresponding Function and specialize in it without interfering and meddling with the other Structures. The relevant specialized Structures for performing the Input and Output functions are the following[55]: (i) Political Socializers are to perform the Function of Political Socialization, (ii) Mass-media are to perform the Function of Political Communication, (iii) Pressure-Groups are to perform the Function of Interest-Articulation, (iv) Political-Parties are to perform the Function of Interest-Aggregation, (v) Legislature is to perform the Function of Rule-Making, (vi) Executive is to perform the Function of Rule-Application, and (vii) Judiciary is to perform the Function of Rule-Adjudication. All these Structures are required to be formed, and each Structure must specialize and perform its corresponding specific Function only and exclusively without interfering or meddling with other Structures. Thus, the parameter of Differentiation includes the variable of Differentiation among the Structures with autonomy as necessary to enable each to perform its specific function, and to specialize in it. In this context, the Development Indices are: (i) greater extent of Structural-Differentiation and Autonomy, and (ii) greater degree of Functional-Specialization and Specificity. This Pattern of Structural-Functional Relationship would make for the increased Capacity of the Political System to perform and to deliver. Hence, the greater is the extent of Structural-Differentiation including Functional-Specialization, the greater may be the level of Development of a Political System. Of course, this developed pattern of 'Structural-Functional Relationship' must not be misconstrued as fragmentation and isolation of the Structures but as specialization based on an ultimate sense of integration of the Political System with a high level of performance-capacity.

Conjointness of the Parameters

The Parameters of Political-Development as postulated in the "Development Syndrome" are, indeed, interrelated and con-joint. The parameter of Equality, the parameter of Capacity and the parameter of Differentiation are interrelated in the sense that one influences and reinforces the other. For instance, a high level of Capacity would likely produce a high level of Equality and, also, a high level of Differentiation; and it may so happen in respect of each Parameter. Hence, all these three Parameters along with the Development-Indices of each may be empirically investigated conjointly in the context of the dynamics of a Political System; and accordingly, the level of its Political Development may be ascertained. Moreover, while investigating into the Phenomenon of Political Development, it becomes imperative to enquire into and analyze the ability of the Political System to resolve successfully the Crises of Political-Development encountered by it is the process of its political evolution. This is imperative because a Political System may attain the 'Developed-Status' only when the Crises of Political-Development are successfully resolved in its life-process.

Crises of Political Development

A National Political Society, in its life-process, encounters six major Crises, what may be termed as the Crises of Political Development.[56] These Crises are: (i) Identity Crisis, (ii) Legitimacy Crisis, (iii) Penetration Crisis, (iv) Participation Crisis, (v) Integration Crisis, and (vi) Distribution Crisis. These Crises may emerge, and be faced by the Political System at different stages during its life-process, and are required to be successfully solved so as to attain the developed-status.

The first and most fundamental crisis is the Identity Crisis which pertains to the problem of creating and achieving a common sense of national identity. The people of the State or Political Society are required to form and develop in themselves a common sense of oneness on recognizing their national territory as their true homeland, and feeling proud of being its members and inhabitants. Simultaneously, they must be prepared to sacrifice or suppress all their parochial identities relating to ethnicity, race, tribe, caste, religion, language etc., if necessary, as and when these conflict or compete with their larger national identity. Such a high sense of national-identity or nationalism would create national unity and integration, and would help-build a stable Nation-State.

Closely related to the Identity Crisis is the Legitimacy Crisis that pertains to the problem of achieving agreement among the people on the legitimate nature of the Government and its Incumbents who are entrusted with the task of governing the Political Society in accordance with its Constitution. People are required to legitimize the Constitution which contains the laws, rules, and procedures of governance, and thus, recognize the agreed form of political life and rules of the political game. The legitimization of the 'Political-Regime' including the Structure of Government, the Procedure of Governance, and the Incumbents of Authority would create in the people favourable psychology and supportive behaviour towards the Political System, and would make it stable and viable.

The legitimized Political System would enact and implement public policies, and thereby, would strive to reach the people who inhabit in different parts of its territory; and thus, it tends to address itself to resolve the Penetration Crisis. As such, it tends to penetrate into every nook and corner of its territory, and to make its presence felt for all its people. The goal is to orient the people towards its policies and activities, and thereby, to obtain their confidence and support. This endeavour for penetration would form a sense of belonging in the people towards the Political System;

and simultaneously, it would help-maintain peace and order in its territory, and pave for its stability and viability.

The fourth crisis of Political Development is the Participation Crisis which needs to be addressed to, and successfully resolved. For obtaining people's legitimacy and support, the Political System is required to provide opportunities and awareness to the people for their active and spontaneous participation and involvement in its political process. Hence, it must champion the values of political liberty and equality, and create necessary institutional arrangement including a free and fair System of Election based on the principle of Universal Adult Franchise, a Competitive Party-System and a System of Pressure-Groups, and a set of inviolable Fundamental Rights that would facilitate people's active, free and voluntary participation in the political process. As such, the resolution of the Participation Crisis may generate a high sense of belongingness in the people towards the Political System, and would foster their supportive behaviour; and hence, it would make for its greater stability and viability.

The next crisis which the Political System faces is the Integration Crisis which involves the problem of integrating all its Structures on tuning them to the national interests and objectives. In this context, of course, the resolution of the preceding Participation Crisis seems to contribute a lot because it creates allegiant-citizenry. Simultaneously, the Political System is required to socialize the people including the Incumbents of all Input and Output Structures in the values of nationalism and patriotism through various governmental and non-governmental agencies. As a consequence, not only the people would stand united and integrated but also all structures of the Political System may become integrated and work together for attainment of national interest and objectives. Thus, the Political System becomes strengthened, and it enjoys a large measure of stability and viability.

The final crisis of Political Development that a Political System encounters in its life-process in the Distribution Crisis. It involves the problem of equitable distribution of goods and services of the

Political Society among the people. Since the Political System is, in reality, a system of political co-existence of the people, by the people, and for the people, it is expected to deliver benefits to all segments of the population by way of enacting and implementing welfare public policies. In this context, welfare-oriented public policies aimed at equitable distribution of societal resources would keep the people contented and satisfied. As such, people's satisfaction would generate system-allegiant orientation in them, and would induce them to undertake supportive behaviour towards the Political System. Thus, on acquiring people's spontaneous support, the Political System would be greatly strengthened, and would remain stable and viable through time.

These Crises, however, arise normally in the life-process of a Political Society, one after the other, in the sequence that commences with the Identity Crisis, and is followed respectively with the Legitimacy Crisis, the Penetration Crisis, the Participation Crisis, the Integration Crisis, and the Distribution Crisis. Successful resolution of these Crises would make the Political System greatly stable and viable, and would help-develop its capacity to perform effectively for attainment of its goals and objectives. As a consequence, the Political System is enabled to display and exhibit the Indices of Political-Development in respect of the Parameters of Equality, Capacity, and Differentiation. It would, thus, attain a 'Developed-Status'. However, the ability of the Political System to resolve these Crises successfully tends to be crucially affected by the pattern of 'Political Culture' of its people.

Political Culture and Political Development

The pattern of 'Political Culture' of the people of a National Society seems to be the most vital determinant of the level of its Political-Development.[57] The tremendous importance of the Political Culture as the vital determinant of Political Development derives from the fact that it constitutes the psychological foundation of a Political System. For attaining the 'Developed-Status', the Political System needs to remain greatly stable and viable, through time, with effective capability to perform and deliver in the context of realization of its goals and objectives. It may be attained successfully provided the Crises of Political-Development are effectively resolved. However, the effective resolution of these Crises tends to depend mostly on people's allegiance and willing support towards the Political System, and it, in turn, tends to be conditioned by their Pattern of Political Culture. Since, the Political Culture of the people characterizes their mindset or psychology, and tends to shape and condition their socio-political behaviour and roles, no Political System may, for long, remain stable and viable with effective capacity to perform without people's allegiance and support. Hence, on acquiring people's spontaneous support born out of their 'Allegiantly-Participant Pattern of Political Culture', what Gabriel A. Almond terms as 'The Civic Culture', the Political System of a National Society may be greatly enabled to resolve the Crises of Political-Development successfully, and there by, it would attain the 'Developed-Status' invested and adorned with the attributes or indices of Political-Development.

A Critical Appraisal

Among the various perspectives and theoretical formulations on the Political Development Phenomenon, the one which is recognized and widely-used by a large number of scholars as the most coherent and comprehensive Theory of Political Development seems to be the 'Development-Syndrome'. However, it seems to be politically biased and prejudiced. On critical scrutiny, it may be noted that the indices and attributes of Political Development, as postulated in the 'Development-Syndrome', are identical with the Values and Principles of Liberal Democracy such as the Values of Liberty, Political Equality, Rationality, Universality, Secularity, and the Principles of Governmental Responsiveness, and Separation of Powers. All these basic Liberal-Democratic Values and Principles are found to be contained in the Parameters of Equality, Capacity, and Differentiation that, together, constitute the Development-Syndrome. Hence, the use and employment of the Development-

Syndrome for measuring the level of Political-Development of a National Society which does not champion and subscribe to the ideology of Liberal Democracy would culminate in characterizing its Political System as an underdeveloped or undeveloped one. As such, all non-democratic Political Systems which operate in Asia, Africa, Latin-America, Middle-East, and Eastern Europe would be assessed as undeveloped Political Systems. Such an assessment, therefore, smacks of politico-cultural biases and prejudices against a large number of Political Systems of the World. It only favours a few Anglo-American Political Systems, and presents them as the Developed Systems. As such, the 'Development-Syndrome' that provides the Model of Political Development for emulation and approximation is found to be 'Culture-bound' in the sense of being bound or limited to the Political Culture and Structural-Arrangement of Liberal Democracy. This short-coming of the 'Development-Syndrome', however, must not reduce or belittle its significance as a great and relevant Theory of Political-Development. What is needed is its refinement in order to make it universally acceptable. It may be noticed that the 'Development-Syndrome's Parameter of Equality which tends to influence and condition the Parameter of Capacity and the Parameter of Differentiation needs to focus not merely on Political Equality guaranteed by the Constitution but also on substantive Socio-Economic Equality of the people because Political Equality without substantive Socio-Economic Equality is a myth; and simultaneously, without substantive Socio-Economic Equality, the provision of Political Equality also becomes a myth. As such, it becomes necessary that the people of the Society must be ensured Liberty and Equality, in reality, in all dimensions of Socio-Political Life, free from exploitation and violence, so that there would prevail substantive Political Equality which, in turn, may promote for the acquisition of greater Capacity and Differentiation by the Political System. For establishing Socio-Political Equality, there must be brought about Economic Development along with equitable distribution of societal resources; and simultaneously, moral values of peace, non-violence, non-exploitation, co-operation, and fraternity need to be inculcated in the people. Consequently, there may be established a Political Society composed of free, autonomous, equal, and morally-conscious individuals who work together selflessly for the attainment of the ultimate goal of an objectively-good life that befits Human-beings on this Earth. Hence, it seems necessary that the level of Political Development of a National Society ought to be fairly judged and assessed, not on the basis of the Ideology of Liberal Democracy as enshrined in the 'Theory of Development-Syndrome', but on the basis of the Parameters of Human-Development that would include both material and moral development of Mankind. The indices of Human Development may, accordingly, be discerned, and a holistic Theory of Political Development needs to be designed for assessing and ascertaining the level of Development of a National Political System.

Notes

1. David Easton (1953). *The Political System: An Inquiry into the State of Political Science.* New York: Alfred K. Knopf. Indian Edition: Calcutta: Scientific Book Agency, 1971, p. 129.
2. Lucian W. Pye (1972). (i) *Aspects of Political Development.* Boston: Little, Browm & Co. Indian Edition, 1996, New Delhi: Amerind Publishing Co. (ii) *Communication and Political Development.* Princeton: Princeton University Press, 1963. Indian Edition: New Delhi: Radha Krishan Prakashan, 1972. (iii) *Political Culture and Political Development.* Edited with Sidney Verba. Princeton: Princeton University Press, 1965. (iv) *Crises and Sequences of Political Development.* Co-authored with Leonard Binder, James S. Coleman, Joseph La Palombara, Sidney Verba and Myron Weiner. Princeton: Princeton University Press, 1971.
3. (i) *The Politics of Developing Areas.* Edited with Gabriel A. Almond. Princeton: Princeton University Press, 1968. (ii) *Education and Political Development.* Edited. Princeton: Princeton University Press, 1965. (iii) "The Development Syndrome", in *Crises and Sequences in Political Development.* Co-authored with Leanard Binder, Joseph La-Palombara, Lucian W. Pye, Sidney Verba, and Myron Weiner, *Op. cit.*

4. Myron Weiner (1971). *Crises and Sequences in Political Development.* Co-authored with Leonard Binder, James S. Coleman, Joseph La-Palombara, Lucian W. Pye, and Sidney Verba. Princeton: Princeton University Press.
5. Joseph La Palombara. (i) *Bureaucracy and Political Development.* Edited. Princeton: Princeton University Press 1964. (ii) *Political Parties and Political Development.* Edited with Myron Weiner. Princeton: Princeton University Press, 1966. (iii) *Crises and Sequences in Political Development.* Co-authored with Leonard Binder, James S. Coleman, Lucian W. Pye, Sidney Verba, and Myron Weiner, *Op. cit.*
6. Leonard Binder. *Crises and Sequences in Political Development.* Co-authored with James S. Coleman, Joseph LaPalombara , Lucian W. Pye, Sidney Verba, and Myron Weiner, *Op. cit.*
7. Samuel P. Huntington (1968). *Political Order in Changing Societies.* New Haven: Yale University Press.
8. Paul A. Baran (1957). *The Political Economy of Growth.* New York: Monthly Review Press.
9. Benjamin Higgins (1959). *Economic Development—Principles, Problems and Policies.* New York: W.W. Norton.
10. David E. Apter (1965). *The Politics of Modernization.* Chicago: Chicago University Press.
11. Walt W. Rostow (1960). *The Stages of Economic Growth.* Cambridge: Cambridge University Press.
12. S. M. Lipset (1960). *Political Man.* London: William Heinemann.
13. K.H. Silvert (1964). *Expectant Peoples—Nationalism and Development.* New York: Random Howa.
14. Clifford Geertz (1963). *Old Societies and New States*, ed. New York: Free Press of Glencoe.
15. Rupert Emerson (1960). *From Empire to Nation.* Cambridge: Harvard University Press.
16. Karl W. Deutsch. (i) *The Nerves of Government: Models of Political Communication and Control.* New York: The Free Press of Glencoe, 1963. (ii) "Social Mobilization and Political Development", *American Political Science Review*, 55, September, 1961.
17. Fred W. Riggs (1964). *Administration in Developing Countries: The Theory of Prismatic Society.* Boston: Houghton Mifflin Co.
18. Max F. Millikan (1961). *The Emerging Nations.* Boston: Little, Brown, Co-authored with Donald L.M. Blackman.
19. Daniel Lerner (1958). *The Passing of Traditional Society.* New York: Free Press of Glencoe.

20. Lucian W. Pye (1972). *Aspects of Political Development.* Indian Edition. New Delhi, Amerind Publishing Co., *Op. cit.* pp. 33-45.
21. Lucian W. Pye. *Ibid.*, pp. 35-45.
22. Paul A. Baren. *The Political Economy of Growth. Op. cit.*
23. Norman S. Buchanan (1955). *Approaches to Economic Development.* Co-authored with Howard S. Ellis. New York: The Twentieth Century Fund.
24. Benjamin Higgins. *Economic Development. Op. cit.*
25. Barbara Ward (1962). *The Rich Nations and the Poor Nations.* London: Hamish Hamilton.
26. Walt W. Rostow. *The Stages of Economic Growth. Op. cit.*
27. David E. Apter. *The Politics of Modernization. Op. cit.*
28. James S. Coleman. (i) *The Politics of Developing Areas. Op. cit.* (ii) *Education and Political Development. Op. cit.*
29. Seymour Martin Lipset. *Political Man. Op. cit.*
30. Karl W. Deutsch. (i) *The Nerves of Government, Op. cit.* (ii) *Social Mobilization and Political Development. Op. cit.*
31. K.H. Silvert. *Expectant People's Nationalism and Development. Op. cit.*
32. Edward Shills (1962). *Political Development in the New States.* The Hague: Mouton.
33. William McCord (1965). *The Springtime of Freedom: Evolution of Developing Societies.* New York: Oxford University Press.
34. Max Weber (1947). *The Theory of Social and Economic Organization.* Translated by A.M. Handerson and Talcott Parsons. Glencoe: The Free Press.
35. Joseph LaPalombara. *Bureaucracy and Political Development* (ed.) *Op. cit.*
36. Clifford Geertz. *Old Societies and New States* (ed.), *Op. cit.*
37. Robert Emerson. *From Empire to Nation, Op. cit.*
38. Bert F. Hoselitz (1952). *The Progress of Underdeveloped Areas* (ed), (Chicago: Chicago University Press.
39. Joseph LaPalombara. (i) *Bureaucracy and Political Development,* (ed.). *Op. cit.* (ii) *Political Parties and Political Development.* (ed.) with Myron Weiner. *Op. cit.* (iii) *Crises and Sequences in Political Development.* Co-authored, *Op. cit.*
40. Karl W. Deutsch. (i) *The Nerves of Government: Models of Political Communication and Control, Op. cit.* (ii) *Social Mobilization and Political Development, American Political Science Review, Op. cit.*
41. Fred. W. Riggs. *Administration in Developing Countries, Op. cit.*
42. James S. Coleman. (i) The "Development Syndrome" in *Crises and Sequences in Political Development, Op. cit.* (ii) *The Politics of Developing*

Areas, Edited with Gabriel A. Almond, *Op. cit.* (iii) *Education and Political Development. Op. cit.*

43. Gabriel A. Almond. (i) "Introduction: A Functional Approach to Comparative Politics", in *The Politics of Developing Areas with James S. Coleman. Op. cit.* (ii) "Political Systems and Political Change", in the *American Behavioural Scientist*, Vol. VI, June, 1963. (iii) *Comparative Politics: A Developmental Approach.* Co-authored with G.B. Powell Jr. Boston: Little Brown & Co., 1966 (iv) *The Civic Culture*, Co-authored with Sidney Verba. Princeton: Princeton University Press, 1963.
44. S. N. Eisenstadt (966). (i) "Breakdown of Modernization" in *Economic Development and Cultural Change*, Vol. XII, No. 2 (July, 1964) (ii) *Modernization: Protest and Change.* Englewood Cliffs, N.J.: Prentice-Hall.
45. Max F. Millikan (1961). *The Emerging Nations.* Co-authored with Donald L.M. Blackmer. Boston: Little Brown & Co.
46. Daniel Lerner (1958). *The Passing of Traditional Society.* New York: Free Press of Glencoe.
47. Lucian W. Pye. *Aspects of Political Development.* Indian Edition, *Op. cit*, p. 45
48. Lucian W. Pye. (i) *Ibid.*, p. 45. (ii) Also, "Foreword" in *Crisis and Sequence in Political Development. Op. cit.*
49. Lucian W. Pye. *Aspects of Political Development,* Indian Edition, *Op. cit.*, pp. 45-48.
50. Lucian W. Pye. *Ibid.*, pp. 45-46.
51. Lucian W. Pye. *Ibid.*, pp. 46-47.
52. Gabriel A. Almond. *Comparative Politics: A Developmental Approach, Op. cit.*, p. 29.
53. Gabriel A. Almond. "An Introduction: A Functional Approach to Comparative Politics" in the *Politics of Developing Areas, Op. cit.*, pp. 11, 18.
54. Gabriel A. Almond. "Introduction: A Functional Approach to Comparative Politics" in the *Politics of Developing Areas, Op. cit.*, p. 17.
55. Gabriel A. Almond. *Ibid.*, pp. 26-58.
56. Lucian W. Pye. (i) *Aspects of Political Development*, Indian Edition, *Op. cit.*, pp. 62-67. (ii) *Crises and Sequences in Political Development, Op. cit.*
57. Gabriel A. Almond. *The Civic Culture, Op. cit.*

10

Epilogue

Modern Political Analysis undertaken on employing Modern Theories and Models seems to be flaw-ridden as it contains some serious shortcomings and limitations. For approximating the Pure-Sciences, it champions and follows the scientific premises of factual analysis, objective analysis, and causal analysis. Accordingly, it involves the employment of scientific methods for the purpose of factual-data collection from observed and observable political phenomena. Simultaneously, the collected data are subjected to objective analysis, free from the value-biases of the Analyst, in order to find out the causal factors, and to explain the phenomena scientifically. These academic endeavours, indeed, are intended to uphold and enrich "The Science of Politics", and may be considered as great intellectual contributions. However, on critical scrutiny, they are found to be socially irrelevant because of some grave shortcomings and limitations inherent in the Behavioural Approach and its concomitant Modern Political Theories that provide guidelines and directions for undertaking Modern Political Analysis.

Limitation of the Behavioural Approach

The Behavioural Approach, in following the footprints of Pure-Sciences, champions the principles of Value-Fact Dichotomy, and the Principles of S-O-R Co-relationship. It requires that the endeavour for theorization and analysis must be based only on observed and observable political facts, and that the Analyst must be value-free (neutral and objective) in collecting and analyzing empirical data. As such, there must be ensured a rigid separation of facts from values as there is no place for values and subjective preferences in scientific analysis of phenomena. However, this Principle of Value-Fact Dichotomy cannot be rigidly applied and adhered to, in reality, by the Social Scientists including the Political Scientists because the Analysts are human beings, and the objects of analysis are human behaviour and roles in socio-political context. As such, value-free political analysis is neither possible nor desirable. It is not possible because the Analyst is primarily a human being who has been born in a family and grown up in a social environment with a distinct pattern of socio-cultural ethos. On being a member of his family and also his Society, he has already been socialized into a distinct pattern of values and cultural ethos that constitute an integral part of his personality. His value-pattern is not external to him like his coat so that he would take it out from his body as and when required, put it on the hanger, and undertake analysis of the political phenomenon. Since his value-pattern is an integral part of his personality and psychology, he can never make himself free from it in undertaking his academic endeavours in collecting and analyzing factual data. Thus, his value-system would inadvertently and inevitably influence his academic endeavours in the context of selection of the research problem, and collection and analysis of the relevant data even if he ardently intends to become completely objective and value-free. Hence, value-free Political Analysis is an impossible proposition. As David Easton emphatically points out: "... We cannot shed our values in the way we remove our coats. Values are an integral part of personality and as long as we are human, we can assume that these mental sets and preferences will be with us. The ideal of a value-free social science has revealed itself as a chimera. Even where a research worker should claim utter impartiality, there can be no doubt that he has simply driven his moral values underground that even he himself may no longer be aware of them."[1] Similarly, Mulford Sibley[2] also affirms that selection of a political phenomenon for research, and its findings would inevitably be influenced, to a great extent, by the researchers 'framework of value judgement' that has been formed in him as a consequence of the impact of his societal culture as to whether it is characterized Liberal, Authoritarian, Anarchic or Marxian values and ethos. Hence, he asserts: "The behaviour of the Behaviouralist can never be value-free"[3] because his "overall view of life-experience constitutes both an evaluation or aesthetic insight and a judgement of fact."[4]

Simultaneously, value-free Political Analysis is also undesirable because, if it becomes value-free or neutral, it would become irrelevant for the Society. The Analyst, in undertaking the analysis of political phenomena, is expected to benefit mankind by way of issuing value-judgements and prescriptions as to what is good or bad, right or wrong, just or unjust, and praiseworthy or condemnable. Because the Analyst is an intellectual and a specialist, he has an obligation to protect and promote the human values of civilization by way of making the people and the policy-makers aware of these. Accordingly, he is expected to issue value-prescriptions for solving the socio-political problems on upholding human-values for the benefit of Mankind.[5] Therefore, if he refrains himself from issuing value-judgements and opinions for becoming objective and scientific at par with Natural Scientists, people would be deprived of his wise-counsels, and as such, his intellectual exercises would become irrelevant for the people of the Society. On the contrary, value-prescriptions issued by the Political Analysts would enlighten the people who, on being provided with a pool of alternative value-prescriptions, would get an opportunity to make a choice for attaining the best kind of political life and existence. As Mulford Sibley rightly points out: "...Politics involves the shaping of Politics, and policies in turn necessitate choices among contesting value-systems"[6], and for becoming socially relevant, "the researcher is expected to laydown guidelines for policy-making."[7] Thus, the Principle of Value-Fact Dichotomy of the Behavioural Approach to the study of Politics is both impossible and undesirable because, as David Easton rightly points out, "...values are inextinguishable parts of the study of politics."[8]

As regards the Principle of S-O-R (Stimulus-Organism-Response) Co-relationship of the Behavioural Approach that requires to enquire into, and ascertain the causal factors of political behaviour, it seems to contain a stupendous difficulty for collecting and analyzing factual data. Individual's political behaviour, in reality, is embedded or rooted in his mindset or psychological which is shaped and conditioned by numerous variables including his Biology, Sociology, Economy, and Ecology. These variables are so many in number that these become extremely difficult to be precisely identified and listed; and at the same time, some of these vital explanatory variables are qualities, not quantities, and hence, these defy quantitative and precise measurement.[9] Moreover, it is extremely difficult to discuss and delineate human psychology because Man is a very complex and complicated creature in whom there may exist no co-relationship in what he thinks, what he says, and what he does. His overt behaviour or responses cannot be reliably analyzed and ascertained because of the lack of true, relevant, and adequate data.[10] Therefore, the Behavioural Political Scientist, as Mulford Sibly[11] also points out, is incapable of providing universally valid scientific predictions concerning political behaviour of individuals and institutions. He may only provide some generalized assumptions which may be true or not in reality because the objects are living human beings with dynamic and ever-changing psychology.[12] Since the Analyst cannot enter and fathom into the psychology of Man, true and reliable data are very difficult to be collected; and the lack of reliable data means the lack of scholarly scientific analysis as the findings would become misleading and erroneous.

Moreover, the Behavioural Approach seems to be misleading in its generalization of findings at the Micro-level to Macro-level. Since it is exclusively concerned with micro-studies at the level of the individuals or groups, and tends to extend the findings to the Society as a whole, these may be untrue and inconsistent with the Macro Socio-Political Realities; and hence, may be misleading and fallacious. As Heinz Eulau rightly points out: "... there is the fallacy of extrapolation from micro to macro phenomena. Small systems are treated as analogues of large systems, and the findings on micro-level are extended to the macro level."[13]

Thus, it may be noted that the Behavioural Approach to Political Analysis is gravely flaw-ridden because of its rigid scientism that involves hyper-factualism, objective precision, and causalism. As a consequence, the purely behavioural or scientific analyses of Politics are found to be sterile, abstruse, and socially irrelevant even if these are presented as the outcome of great intellectual exercises, and are couched in esoteric jargons and pompous words. These shortcomings and limitations of the Behavioural Approach were noticed and focused greatly during the period from 1960 to 1970 when Modern Political Analysis and Theories failed disastrously to solve the then pressing problems[14] of mankind the world-over. During this period, there emerged, in the domestic arena of a number of States, the problems of unrelenting Civic-unrest; Students-agitations; rise of Political Authoritarianism and Dictatorial-rule; Loss of Human Rights, Decline of the Human Values of Liberty, Equality, Justice and Fraternity; Widespread Poverty, Unemployment and Economic-inflation; and in the international arena, there emerged the Scenario of Cold-war, Inter-state Conflicts; and the Proliferation of Nuclear-weapons that endangered world peace and order. These emerging problems could not be satisfactorily addressed, and solved by the Behavioural Political Scientists through their Modern Political Analyses and Theorization. Consequently, the Behavioural or purely Scientific Analyses of Politics were found to be merely the outcome of ivory-tower intellectual exercises, and hence, socially irrelevant; and there was felt the need to bring out necessary reforms in the Behavioural Approach on organizing a new intellectual movement, what Easton termed as 'the Post-behavioural Revolution'[15] in the discipline of Political Science.

The Post-Behavioural Movement

For becoming socially relevant, the pressing need of a new orientation to political research and analysis was emphatically pointed out by David Easton in his Presidential Address to the American Political Science Association in 1969. His address focused on the emerging dissatisfaction of a large number of Political Scientists as to the inadequacy of the Behavioural Approach; and simultaneously, on their demands for bring out necessary reforms in order to make the academic endeavours for Political Analysis and Theorization socially relevant and useful. As such, in responding positively to this need of the time, there emerged, from 1969 onwards, the Post-behavioural Movement with the prime aim of checking the Decline of Political Theory and Analysis into pure scientific empiricism, and simultaneously, of making socially relevant intellectual endeavours in this context. As David Easton puts it, the Post-Behavioural Movement emerged because of 'a deep dissatisfaction' with the behavioural political approach that strove to make "the study of politics into a more rigorously scientific discipline modelled on the methodology of the natural sciences"[16]; and simultaneously, it intended to propel Political Science in new directions so as to make it socially relevant on reaching to the real needs of mankind.[17] As such, it is essentially characterized with the "Credo of Relevance"[18] that postulates some salient tenets as guidelines for undertaking Post-behavioural Theorization and Analysis. In this context, the most important tenet is, as Easton puts it: "Substance must precede technique"[19], because "it is more important to be relevant and meaningful to contemporary urgent social problems than to be sophisticated in the tools of investigation."[20] He points out that the prime goal of our intellectual activities must be 'Service to mankind' by way of reaching out to their real needs, and of help-solving their pressing socio-economic and political problems. Hence, there must be avoided ivory-tower intellectual exercises unrelated to the ground realities of life; and also, rigid adherence to the scientific principles of value-fact dichotomy as well as the scientific techniques and methods of data collection and analysis. Since we are concerned with human beings and human problems, we must desist from being value-free, and we must refrain ourselves from becoming like the 'Pure Scientists' of Natural Sciences.

For making our intellectual endeavours socially relevant, what is needed is adherence to the tenet of 'Value-Fact-Association' in the sense that value must be restored to its central position in political research, and that value-judgements must be proposed by the researchers even though empirical fact would constitute the basis of research. As David Easton[21] points out, the Post-Behavioural Approach deplores only the technical excesses in research but it recognizes the necessity of scientific techniques and methods of factual data-collection and analysis that the Behavioural Approach champions and upholds. The Behavioural Approach which is characterized with pure-scientism, and which, as such, is exclusively concerned with description and explanation devoid of value-prescription is, thus, reformed by way of limiting the technological excesses of pure scientific analysis, and of including in it the provision for issuing value-prescriptions. Hence, the Post-behavioural Approach recognizes the necessity of the techniques and method of the Behavioural Approach in the context of factual data-collection and analysis, but it rejects rigid adherence to them; and for making political analyses socially relevant, it requires the Political Scientists to address themselves to value-questions, and to prescribe ethical goals for the benefit of mankind. Thus, the Post-Behavioural Approach combines the scientific necessity for factual analysis with the social necessity for issuing ethical (value) prescriptions. As David Easton emphatically points out: "The basic premises of pure sciences are not to be abandoned but be compromised and combined with the need for social relevance"[22], and hence, the Political Scientists need to be involved in scholarly-endeavours for value-construction without relinquishing the scientific basis of analyzing the phenomena.

Moreover, for becoming socially relevant, the Political Scientist is required, along with his prescription of ethical goals, to act actively to improve political life according to human criteria and the values of civilization. As David Easton points out: "Knowledge brings an awareness of alternatives and their consequences... The political scientist as a professional is the knower par excellence... to know, to bear the responsibility for acting."[23] As an expert on socio-political issues, the Political Scientist must use his expert knowledge, through active action, for bringing about social reforms for the good of mankind. In order to fulfil this obligation, as Easton suggests, there must take place 'politicization of the profession'[24] through formation of Professional Associations. Since, values are inextinguishable part of the study of Politics[25], the Political Scientists are expected to point out what is desirable on policy-issues, and to enlighten and guide the people as well as the policy-makers for protection and promotion of human well-being and civilizational values.[26] Of course, addition of values to factual analysis does not mean a return to the utopian speculation of the Political Philosopher. Basing on scientifically collected and analyzed data on empirical political phenomena, value-prescriptions need to be provided by the post-behaviourally oriented Political Scientists for fulfilling their social obligations actively and meaningfully. Hence, there must be designed scientifically-based socially relevant theories so that the analysis of empirical political phenomena may be undertaken for the benefit of mankind. As David Easton emphatically points out: "We require boldly speculative theorizing that is prepared to build upon rather than to reject the findings of contemporary behavioural science itself and that is prepared to contemplate the implications of these findings for political life in the light of alternative, articulate value-frameworks."[27] These Theories and Models, thus designed, would provide guidelines for undertaking systematic, coherent, socially relevant, and meaningful analysis of political phenomena.

This newly emerging pattern of political analysis is the intellectual outcome of the Post-behavioural Approach that champions the principle of Value-Fact Association for becoming socially relevant. It is the central focus, and also, the seminal contribution of the Post-behavioural Movement that heralds a distinct and distinguishing intellectual tendency for undertaking Political Analysis. Hence, David Easton rightly describes the Post-behavioural Movement as "a genuine revolution, not a reaction, a becoming, not a preservation, a reform, not a counter-reformation."[28]

Contemporary Trends

The Post-behavioural Approach launches some distinct intellectual trends, what may be termed as Contemporary Trends of Political-Theorization and Analysis. These may be discerned and delineated as the following:

(i) Search for Scientific-Empiricism.
(ii) Search for Comprehensiveness.
(iii) Search for Social-Relevance.
(iv) Search for Value-laden Micro-Intellectual Orders based on Multi-Culturalism.

The Search for Scientific-Empiricism requires that research must be undertaken on the basis of actual political facts collected and analyzed on using scientific techniques and methods. These empirical data must relate to all components of the Political System so that the Politics of the Society may be studied, analyzed, and comprehended comprehensively. Simultaneously, these empirical data must relate to the patterns of culture of various groups of people of the concerned Political-Society. The Society is characterized by multi-culturalism as it is composed of varieties of groups with distinct identities and behaviour-patterns in terms of the socio-cultural variables of race, ethnicity, gender, caste, tribe, language, religion, class, income, occupation, education etc. As such, the cultural-ethos and issues of each of these groups tend to determine, to a very great extent, the roles of the individual and the groups in context the dynamics of the Political-Society. Hence, for understanding Politics of the Society adequately, the cultural-ethos of these groups must be made the basic of analysis; and the research work must contain socially useful and beneficial value-prescriptions for the good of mankind. Of course, these micro-studies must be specific to the individual or concerned group, and must not be generalized to the macro socio-political phenomena. Moreover, basing on these empirical findings and prescriptions, micro-intellectual orders or 'Theories and Models' need to be designed as these would provide useful guidelines for undertaking further research-works that would facilitate the process of reinforcement or refinement or rejection of the prevalent theories, and of building of new theories on the basis of current findings. This new role of the Political Scientist is also emphatically pointed out by Gabriel A. Almond as he opines: "Practical judgment of good and evil in the area of public policy is the special responsibility of the social scientist."[29] Similarly, Arnold Brecht also states: 'It is the function of the political theorist to see soon than others, and to analyze more profoundly than others, the immediate and potential problems of the political life of the society, to supply the practical politician, well in advance with alternative courses of action, the foreseeable consequences of which have been fully thought through, and to supply him not only with brilliant asides, but with a solid block of knowledge on which to build."[30]

Thus, Search for Scientific-Empiricism, Search for Comprehensiveness, Search for Social-Relevance, and Search for Value-laden Micro-Intellectual Order based on Multi-Culturalism tend to signal and characterize the Contemporary-Trends, what may also be termed as the Post-behavioural Trends or the Post-Modern Trends of Political-Theorization and Analyses. These academic pursuits seem to contribute significantly towards the advancement of knowledge in the Discipline of Political Science.

Notes

1. David Easton. *The Political System: An Inquiry into the State of Political Science*. New York: Alfred A. Knopf, 1953, Indian Reprint: Scientific Book Agency, New Delhi, 1971, p. 225.
2. Mulford Sibley (1967). "Limitations of Behaviouralism" in James C. Charlesworth (ed.), *Contemporary Political Analysis*. New York: The Free Press., pp. 51-71, especially p. 54.
3. Mulford Sibley. *Op. cit*, p. 61.
4. *Ibid.*
5. David Easton. "The New Revolution in Political Science", *The American Political Science Review*, Vol. LXIII, No. 4, December, 1969. Reprinted in "The Political System: An Inquiry into the State of Political Science", *Op. cit*, p. 343.
6. Mulford Sibley. *Limitations of Behaviouralism*, *Op. cit*, p. 68.
7. Mulford Sibley. *Op. cit*, p. 68.
8. David Easton. *The New Revolution in Political Science*, *Op. cit.*, p. 326.
9. Jean Blondel (1969). *An Introduction to Comparative Government*. London: Weidenfeld and Nicholson, p. 13.
10. Jean Blondel. *Op. cit*, p. 14.
11. Mulford Sibley. 'Limitations of Behaviouralism' *Op. cit.*, pp. 63-64.
12. Mulford Sibley. *Op. cit*, pp. 63-64.
13. Heinz Eulau. "Segment of Political Science Most Susceptible to Behaviouristic Treatment" in James Charles Worth (ed.) *Contemporary Political Analysis*, *Op. cit*, pp. 33-50, especially, pp. 46-47.
14. David Easton. *The New Revolution in Political Science*, *Op. cit*, pp. 350-53.
15. David Easton. *Op. cit*, p. 323.
16. *Ibid.*, p. 324.
17. *Ibid.*
18. *Ibid.*, p. 325.
19. *Ibid.*
20. *Ibid.*
21. *Ibid.*, p. 330.
22. *Ibid.*, p. 323.
23. *Ibid.*, p. 343.
24. *Ibid.*, p. 345.
25. *Ibid.*, p. 326.
26. *Ibid.*, p. 344.
27. *Ibid.*, p. 340.

28. *Ibid.*, p. 324.
29. Gabriel A. Almond (1946). "Politics, Science and Ethics in Politics and Ethics: A Symposium", *American Political Science Review*, Vol. 40, p. 292.
30. Arnold Brecht (1959). *Political Theory. The Foundation of Twentieth Century Political Thought*. Princeton: Princeton University Press, p. 20.

Bibliography

Agger, Robert E. and Daniel Goldrich, Bert E. Swanson (1964). *The Rulers and the Ruled.* New York: Wiley.

Almond, Gabriel A. and James S. Coleman (1960). *The Politics of Developing Areas.* Princeton, N.J:Princeton University Press.

Almond, Gabriel A. and Sidney Verba (1963). *The Civic Culture-Political Attitudes and Democracy in Five Nations.* Princeton, N.J: Princeton University Press.

Almond, Gabriel A. and G.B. Powell, Jr (1966). *Comparative Politics—A Developmental Approach.* Boston: Little, Brown & Co.

Apter, David E. (1965). *The Politics of Modernization.* Chicago: Chicago University Press.

Aristotle. "The Politics". Translated by Ernest Barker (1969), *The Politics of Aristotle.* New York: Oxford University Press.

Baran, Paul A. (1957). *The Political Economy of Growth.* NewYork: Monthly Review Press.

Barnes, Samuel H. *et al.* (1979). *Political Action-Mass Participation in Five Western Democracies.* Beverly Hills, California: Sage publications.

Bentley, Arthur F. (1908). *The Process of Government.* Chicago: Chicago University.

Blondel, Jean (1969). *An Introduction to Comparative Government.* London: Weidenfeld and Nicholson.

Brecht, Arnold (1959). *Political Theory.* New Jersey: Princeton University Press.

Buchanan, Norman S. and Howard S. Ellis (1955). *Approaches to Economic Development.* New York: Twentieth Century Fund.

Campbell, Angus and Gerald Gurin, Warren B.Miller (1954). *The Voter Decides.* Evanston, Illinois: Row & Peterson.

Campbell, Angus and P.E. Converse, W. Miller, Donald Stokes (1960). *The American Voter.* New York: Wiley.

Charlesworth, James C.(ed.) (1967). *Contemporary Political Analysis.* NewYork: The Free Press.

Catlin, George E. G. (1927). *The Science and Methods of Politics.* New York: Knopf.

Curtis, Michael (1968). *Comparative Government and Politics.* New York: Harper& Row.

Dahl, Robert A. (1961). *Who Governs ?* New Haven: Yale University Press.

_______(1963). *Modern Political Analysis.* Englewood Cliffs, N.J: Prentice-Hall.

_______ (1971). *Polyarchy-Participation and Opposition.* New Haven: Yale University Press.

Davies, James C. (1963). *Human Nature in Politics.* New York: Wiley.

Davies, Morton R. and Vaughan A. Lewis (1971). *Models of Political Systems.* London: Pall Mall Press.

Deutsch, Karl W. (1963). *Nerves of Government—Models of Political Communication and Control.* New York:The Free Press, 1963).

Dyke, Vernon Van (1960). Political Science—A Philosophical Analysis. California: Stanford University Press.

Easton, David (1953). *The Political System—An Inquiry in to the State of Political Science.* New York: Alfred A. Knopf.

_______ (1965). *A Framework for Political Analysis.* Englewood Cliffs, N. J: Prentice-Hall.

_______ (1965). *A Systems Analysis of Political Life.* New York: Wiley.

Eckstein, Harry (1960). *Pressure Group Politics.* Stanford: Stanford University Press.

Eisenstadt, S.N. (1966). *Modernization—Protest and Change.* Englewood Cliffs, N.J: Prentice-Hall.

Emerson, Rupert (1960). *From Empire to Nation.* Cambridge: Harvard University Press.

Eulau, Heinz (1969). *Micro-Macro Political Analysis.* Chicago: Aldine Publishing Co.

Eulau, Heinz and Samuel Eldersveld, Morris Janowitz (eds.) (1956). *Political Behaviour-A Reader*. New York: The Free Press.

Firth, Raymond W. (1961). *Elements of Social Organization*. London: Watts.

Geertz, Clifford (ed.) (1963). *Old Societies and New States*. New York: Free Press.

Goel, M.L. (1975). *Political Participation in a Developing Nation*. New York: Asia Publishing House.

Greenstein, Fred I. (1965). *Children and Politics*. New Haven: Yale University Press.

_______(1969). *Personality and Politics*. Chicago: Markham Publishing Co..

Greenstein, Fred I. and Nelson W. Polsby (eds.) (1975). *Political Science-Tradition, Discipline, Profession, Science, Enterprise*. London: Addison-Welsey.

Greenstein, Fred I, and Michael Lerner (eds.) (1971). *A Source Book for the Study of Personality and Politics*. Chicago: Markham Publishing Co..

Higgins, Benjamin (1959). *Economic Development-Principles, Problems, and Policies*. New York: W.W. Norton.

Hoselitz, Bert F. (ed.) (1952). *The Progress of Underdeveloped Areas*. Chicago: Chicago University Press.

Huntington, Samuel H. (1968). *Political Order in Changing Societies*. New Haven: Yale University Press.

Hunter, Floyd (1963). *Community Power-Structure*. New York: Anchor Books.

Jaros, Dean (1973). *Political Socialization*. New York: Praeger.

Kavanagh, Dennis (1972). *Political Culture*. London: The Macmillan Press.

Key, V.O. Jr (1942). *Politics, Parties and Pressure-Groups*. New York: Thomas-Crowell.

Knertson, JeaneNickel (1972). *The Human Basis of the Polity*. Chicago: Aldine-Atherton.

Lerner, Daniel (1958). *The Passing of Traditional Society*. New York: Free Press.

Lipset, Seymour Martin (1960). *Political Man-Social Bases of Politics*. New York: Double Day.

Lane, Robert E. (1959). *Political Life-Why People Get Involved in Politics*? New York: Free Press.

Lasswell, Harold D. (1950). *Psychopathology and Politics*. Chicago: Chicago University Press.

_______ (1936). *Politics—Who Gets, What, When, How*. New York: McGraw-Hill.

_______(1947). *The Analysis of PoliticalBehaviour—An Empirical Approach*. London: Kegan Paul.

_______ (1948). *Power and Personality*. New York: W.W. Norton.

_______ (1956). *The Decision Process-Seven Categories of Functional Analysis*. Maryland: Maryland University Press.

_______ (1963). *The Future of Political Science*. New York: Atherton Press.

_______ (1971). *A Pre-view of Policy Sciences*. New York: Elsevier Pub.Co.

_______ (1971). *The Policy Orientation of Political Science*. Agra, India: L.N. Agrawal Press .

Lasswell, Harold D. and Abraham Kaplan (1950). *Power and Society-A Framework For Political Analysis*. New Haven: Yale University Press.

Latham, Earl (1952). *The Group Basis of Politics*. New York: Cornell University Press.

MacPherson, C.B. (1962). *The Political Theory of Possessive Individualism*. London: Oxford University Press.

Maslow, Abraham Harold (1954). *Motivation and Personality*. New York: Harpin.

Merriam, Charles E. (1925). *New Aspects of Politics*. Chicago: Chicago University Press.

Mc Cord, William (1965). *The Spring-time of Freedom-Evolution of Developing Societies*. New York: Oxford University Press.

Meadow, R. B. (1960). *Politics as Communication*. Norwood, N.J: Ablex Pub. Co.

Meisel, James S. (1958). *The Myth of the Ruling Class-Gaetano Mosca and the Elites*. Ann Arbor: University of Michigan Press.

Michels, Robert (1942). *Political Parties*. Glencoe, Illinois: Free Press.

Milbrath, Lester W. (1965). *Political Participation-How and Why People Get Involved in Politics*. Chicago: Rand McNally Co.

Moore, W.E. (1953). *Organizational Behaviour*. Princeton, N.J: Princeton Univ. Press.

Mosca, Gaetano (1942). *The Ruling Class. Glencoe*, Illinois: The Free Press.

Olsen, Marvin E. (1968). *The Process of Social Organization*. New York: Holt, Rinehart & Winston.

Palombara, Joseph La (ed.) (1964). *Bureaucracy and Political-Development*. Princeton: Princeton University Press.

Palombara, Joseph La and Myron Weiner (1966). *Political Parties and Political-Development*. Princeton: Princeton University Press.

Pateman, Carole (1970). *Participation and Democratic-Theory*. London: Cambridge-University Press.

Parry, Geraint (1969). *Political Elites*. London: George Allen& Unwin.

Pareto, Vilfredo (1935). *The Mind and Society*. New York: Harcourt-Brace.

Pye, Lucian W. (1965). *Political Culture and Political-Development*. Princeton, N.J: Princeton University Press.

________(1966). *Aspects of Political Development*. Boston: Little, Brown& Co.

Pye, Lucian W. and Sidney Verba (1963). *Communications and Political-Development*. Princeton, N.J: Princeton University Press.

Pye, Lucian W. and Leonard Binder, James S. Coleman, Joseph La Palombara, Sidney Verba, Myron Weiner (1971). *Crises and Sequences of Political Development*. Princeton: Princeton University Press.

Renshon, Stanley Allen (1974). *Psychological Needs and Political-Behaviour-A Theory of Personality and Political Efficacy*. New York: The Free Press.

Riggs Fred W. (1964). *Administration in Developing-Countries-The Theory of Prismatic Society*. Boston: Houghton & Mifflin Co.

Riker, William H. (1964). *The Theory of Political Coalitions*. New Haven: Yale University Press.

Rostow, Walt W. (1960). *The Stages of Economic Growth*. Cambridge: Cambridge University Press.

Schumpeter, Joseph A. (1976). *Capitalism, Socialism and Democracy*. London: Allen & Unwin.

Silvert, K.H. (1964). *Expectant Peoples-Nationalism and Development*. New York: Random House.

Sills, Edward (1962). *Political Development in New States*. Hague: Moufton.

Sills, David L. (1968). *International Encyclopedia of Social Sciences.* New York: The Macmillan & Free Press.

Sniderman, Paul M. (1975). *Personality and Democratic-Politics.* Berkeley: University of California Press.

Simon, Herbert A. and C. Barnard (1947). *Administrative Behaviour.* (New York: Macmillan.

SolaPool, Ithiel D. (ed.) (1967). *Contemporary Political Science-Toward Empirical Theory.* New York: McGraw-Hill.

Truman, David B. (1951). *The Governmental Process.* New York: Alfred Knopf.

Verba, Sidney (1961). *Small Groups and Political-Behaviour.* Princeton: PrincetonUniversity Press.

Verba, Sidney and Noman H. Nie (1972). *Participation in America-Political Democracy and Equality.* New York: Harper & Row.

Wallas, Graham (1908). *Human Nature in Politics.* London: Constable Press.

Ward, Barbara (1962). *The Rich Nations and the Poor* Nations. London: Hamish-Hamilton.

Watkins, Frederick M. (1934). *The State as a Concept of Political Science.* New York: Harper.

Weber, Max (1947). *The Theory of Social and Economic Organization.*
Translated by A.M. Handerson & Talcott Parson. New York: Oxford University Press.

Weiner, Norbert (1956). *The Human Use of Human-Beings.* Garden City, New York: Double Day.

Weissberg, Robert (1974). *Political Learning, Political-Choice, and Democratic-Citizenship.* Englewood Cliffs, N.J: Prentice-Hall.

Wilcox, A.R. (ed.) (1974). *Public Opinion and Political-Attitudes—A Reader.* New York: Wiley.

Wilson, E.K. (1966). *Sociology-Rules, Roles and Relationships.* Illinois: Dorsey Press.

Young, Oran R. (1968). *Systems of Political Science.* Princeton, N.J: Princeton University Press.

Young, Ronald (1958). *Approaches to the Study of Political Science. Evanston.* Illinois: North Western-University Press.

Index